SANCTUARY

SANCTUARY

A Resource Guide
for Understanding and
Participating in the Central
American Refugees' Struggle

Gary MacEoin, Editor

1817

Harper & Row, Publishers, San Francisco
Cambridge, Hagerstown, New York, Philadelphia
London, Mexico City, São Paulo, Singapore, Sydney

SANCTUARY: *A Resource Guide for Understanding and Participating in the Central American Refugees' Struggle.* Copyright © 1985 by Tucson Ecumenical Council Task Force for Central America. "The Refugee" by Elie Wiesel. Copyright © 1985 by Elirion Association, Inc. All rights reserved. Printed in the United States of America. No part of this book may be used or reproduced in any manner whatsoever without written permission except in the case of brief quotations embodied in critical articles and reviews. For information address Harper & Row, Publishers, Inc., 10 East 53rd Street, New York, NY 10022. Published simultaneously in Canada by Fitzhenry & Whiteside, Limited, Toronto.

FIRST EDITION

Library of Congress Cataloging in Publication Data

Sanctuary: a resource guide for understanding and participating in the Central American refugees' struggle.

Papers derived from the Inter-American Symposium on Sanctuary, held in Tucson, Ariz., Jan. 23–24, 1985, and sponsored by the Tucson Ecumenical Council's Task Force for Central America and others.
1. Refugees—Central American—Congresses. 2. Asylum, Right of—Biblical teaching—Congresses. 3. Asylum, Right of—Congresses. I. MacEoin, Gary. II. Inter-American Symposium on Sanctuary (1985: Ariz.) III. Tucson Ecumenical Council. Task Force for Central America.
HV640.5.C46S26 1985   261.8′32   85–45301
ISBN 0-06-065372-8 (pbk.)

---

85 86 87 88 89 10 9 8 7 6 5 4 3 2 1

Sanctuary is the fruit of a two-day Sanctuary Symposium sponsored by the Tucson Ecumenical Council's Task Force for Central America. In addition to the principal presentations of that Symposium, the book contains three important additional elements, a History of the Sanctuary Movement, an Appendix on How to Establish a Sanctuary, and a philosophic and poetic analysis by Dr. Elie Wiesel of what it means to be a refugee. Dr. Wiesel's contribution, which forms the opening chapter, is the edited version of a talk he gave in Tucson, Arizona, on the evening preceding the opening of the Symposium.

CONTENTS

PREFACE
Herb Schmidt

Because of the Civil War in El Salvador, more than one million refugees have been created. More than fifty-one thousand civilians—women, children, and men not involved in the military or with the guerrillas—have been murdered or have disappeared. Thirty-five priests, nuns, and pastors have been assassinated in the last five years. Since President Duarte's election in April 1984, the situation in the cities has changed. The death squads remain intact, but they are being to a considerable extent restrained. Only two hundred fifty death squad assassinations were recorded in 1984, and there were only somewhat more than twelve hundred other killings of noncombatants recorded. But what does not appear in the official lists is the unknown but enormous number of noncombatant old people and children killed by aerial bombardment and in ground sweeps by the Salvadoran army in areas controlled by the popular forces. Such is the basic situation that has forced refugees to flee to "safe haven" in this country. Many of those deported back to their homeland have faced rape, imprisonment, torture, even death. Those are the facts and events that have prompted religious communities to respond by providing sanctuary, as part of the movement that is the subject of this book.

What you will find in this small book is not an academically seasoned, intellectual, dispassionate theological or political discussion of the sanctuary movement. It is, rather, a passionate, involved, soul-searching, intellectually challenging, theologically penetrating, personal expression by scholars, refugees, and sanctuary workers reflecting on the existential struggle to be faithful to our visions of faith with committed action that challenges the oppressive "principalities and powers" of our day. It is our hope that these pages will help many more individuals and faith communities to become aware

1

of the plight of refugees and to join us in seeing that justice and mercy be done in our day.

Last summer a number of us involved in the sanctuary movement in Tucson, Arizona, began dreaming of a symposium to discuss the political, theological, philosophical, legal, and ethical issues involved in providing safe haven for refugees from Central America. Our dreams were modest. We planned to bring together a few theologians, scholars in the humanities, historians, refugees, and sanctuary workers to help us reflect critically on the movement and understand better the implications of our actions, thereby deepening our commitment and involving more religious communities in our efforts. A symposium, we hoped, would state clearly the reality of the refugee situation, namely, that those knocking at our doors are victims of political persecution who, if deported, would be exposed to further suffering. We hoped to make the American public better understand why we feel compelled as an act of conscience to provide sanctuary. In planning our symposium, we were merely following what we had learned from brothers and sisters of faith in Central and South America. The experience of faith communities involved in struggles of liberation had shown us that, following initial reflection and praxis, or committed action, there needs to be a time for further reflection, a time to study the biblical basis and faith foundations that have prompted our actions. These were our modest dreams, and they came true in a way we never expected!

With the help of Gary MacEoin, a noted author and authority on Central America, we began contacting leading theologians, philosophers, historians, and scholars in the humanities. We were overwhelmed by the willingness of so many people to come and share our critical reflection on the sanctuary movement. Our dreams expanded, and we ventured to invite the very best people we could find in North and South America to accompany us in this venture. Much to our surprise, everyone we invited was willing to join us. All who participated served without honoraria and have designated that any proceeds from the sale of this book be given to support the sanctuary movement.

Sanctuary workers from different parts of the country began to respond positively, recognizing the need for in-depth reflection. Almost everyone in the movement knew that it was time to confront

seriously the conflicting theological, ideological, and political positions held by different people in the movement. Sanctuary communities from across the country began to provide financial assistance
so that refugees could participate. We have learned from sisters and
brothers from Central and South America that it is impossible to do
theology or serious faith reflection without involving the very people
who are most affected by the oppression and violence of the civil war
and political persecution in Central America.

More than one hundred sanctuary communities not only resolved
to participate fully in the symposium but also planned a consultation to follow the symposium in which the hard realities of serious
political action in the movement might be discussed and ways be
developed for different local sanctuary communities of faith to better work together.

There was still the financial problem of providing transportation
for so many people and of properly publicizing the event. We were
fortunate to receive grants from national Lutheran, Presbyterian,
and Roman Catholic sources and were gratified that the Arizona
Humanities Council was willing to match those funds so that this
kind of reflection by scholars—and others—could take place.

When the Immigration and Naturalization Service (INS) moved
against sixteen North American sanctuary workers and fifty-three
Central American refugees on 14 January 1985, we knew we were
involved in an event that was truly a *kairos* ("opportune occasion")
in the deepest sense of that Greek word. The symposium became
such a moment, a real breakthrough for us in the sanctuary movement and an opportunity for people in North, Central, and South
America to gain new insight into why faith communities risk providing safe haven. Instead of a few hundred, some fifteen hundred people attended, and the event was covered by the national news media.
Sanctuary communities had new opportunities to witness to the
commitment of faith that has informed their actions, and to describe both the plight of the refugees and the conditions that caused
it. No amount of planning on our part, no amount of financial support, could have given us such an opportunity. The time was right,
and in a real sense, our preparations coincided with God's gracious
action and timing.

The Planning Committee gives special thanks to Tim Nonn, a

seminary intern from the San Francisco Bay Area. Tim did most of the staff coordination for the Inter-american Symposium on Sanctuary held in Tucson, Arizona, 23–24 January 1985. His commitment of time, energy, and enthusiasm made the event possible. We also thank the Arizona Humanities Council and the church bodies that provided the initial funding. We are truly grateful to the Tucson Ecumenical Council's Task Force for Central America, the Office of Hispanic Affairs of the Diocese of Tucson, Temple Emanu-El (Tucson), San Francisco Theological Seminary, the Campus Christian Center, the University of Arizona Religious Studies Program, the University of Arizona Latin American Area Center, and Catholics for Peace and Justice, who all co-sponsored this event. We are especially grateful to Temple Emanu-El and Rabbi Joseph Weizenbaum and his congregation for hosting the conference, and we are deeply indebted to the hundreds of volunteers who worked thousands of hours to make the conference, and this book, a reality.

We hope these presentations will motivate all of us to continue to dream dreams and see new visions so that God's liberating actions can be realized among us as we act on the basis of our faith commitments.

Tucson, Arizona
June 15, 1985

Herb Schmidt for the Planning Committee:
  Jim Corbett
  Ricardo Elford
  John Fife
  Gary MacEoin
  Tim Nonn
  Carla Pedersen
  Joseph Reed
  Marguerite Bowden Reed
  Edwina Vogel
  Joseph Weizenbaum
  Phil Willis-Conger
  Marion Zimmer

PART ONE

Overview

CHAPTER 1

THE REFUGEE
Elie Wiesel

How could I fail to identify with refugees when I myself am one? Yes. I too was a refugee. Something in me is a refugee. In a strange way, a person who has been a refugee remains a refugee.

I'll give you two anecdotal examples. One is that whenever I travel abroad, I don't buy anything, God knows I have no patience, no interest, in buying anything in Paris or London. Yet whenever I return to the United States from abroad, before going through customs, I, quite literally, am afraid. There is nothing to be afraid of but I am afraid, because I am a refugee. As a journalist I crossed many borders, and whenever I had to cross a border, it was hell. I never knew whether I would get in or out of somewhere from somewhere else. Everybody was looking at me suspiciously, because everybody looks at refugees suspiciously.

The second example is as anecdotal as the first, but more dramatic. I drive a car. I don't know how I do it, but I drive. And, believe me, when I got my driver's license, I was prouder than when I got an honorary degree. But when we have to make a U-turn in New York, I am so afraid of the policemen that I stop and let my wife do it.

There is a third beautiful anecdote that I remember from those times, and it is pertinent. In Europe during the war, the refugees passed their time waiting for visas. Always waiting for visas. They would wait for days and days and days, standing in line in front of all kinds of consulates, waiting for a visa to anywhere.

The main thing was to get out, out of occupied France, out of Europe, and to go. Two Jewish people finally managed to get into different consulates, and when they met, one said to the other, "Did you get a visa?" "Yes!" "Where to?" "I'm going to Brazil." "Good." The other person then asked, "And you also got a visa? Where are you going?" The answer was in Spanish: "Tierra del

Fuego." So the other person then said, "But that is so far!" And the first replied "Far from where?"

That, to me, describes the state of mind of a refugee. Far from where? Suddenly geographic distances no longer matter. One can live a mile away from the border, and it's not a mile, it's a lifetime. Those French people who, during the war resided at the Swiss border, for instance, saw Switzerland day after day; they saw people who lived freely. I could never understand them and still cannot . . . what did *they* think of their freedom?

Permit me to turn the question around. I could never understand and I cannot understand now how those people in Switzerland, who were free, could remain free and eat in the morning and at lunch and at dinner while looking at the other side, at occupied France. After all, they lived in the same time, and yet, time itself had its own divisions.

If ever time was a metaphysical notion, that was it: when good and evil were separated by a man-made frontier. Any frontier is man-made, and yet, on one side people died, while on the other they went on living as though the others didn't die.

Those who know me will confirm that I am not a political person. I have never been involved in anything political. I don't understand politics; to me, it is something extremely obscure. I come from a tradition that aims at conferring an ethical meaning on anything a person does or does not do.

I would like, therefore, to see this problem in its ethical perspective. And from the ethical perspective, it is impossible for human beings today, especially for my contemporaries, who have seen what people can do to themselves and to one another, not to be involved. We must be with those who have suffered, and we must be with those who have tried to prevent others from suffering. This is the real community: it does not deny the differences, but rather enhances and transcends them. Because I am a Jew, and profoundly a Jew, I have to be a part of that community.

I have been asking myself where the whole concept of sanctuary comes from. First I went back to the Bible, and I discovered that there the word *sanctuary* somehow is not what we think it is.

The sanctuary concept in Scripture is rooted in what we call in Hebrew *arey miklat*, meaning "cities of refuge." However, we cannot draw a direct parallel. For a refuge-city, according to the Bible, is a place for guilty people, as distinct from refugees fleeing from Central America. A person who inadvertently was guilty, who unwittingly, unknowingly, committed a crime, would flee to one of the designated cities for a safe haven from revenge. Why? We are told in the Bible that it is natural to want to avenge a relative. It is an instinctive reaction. But there is one place where that avenger cannot enter. It is the refuge-city.

So I said to myself, that principle doesn't apply in your case, because surely not one of you has committed any crime. If you are here, my friends, it is because you want to live far from crime. It is because you want to renounce a society that may, in its foolishness, believe that violence is the answer. That is why you are here. And therefore you deserve another kind of sanctuary. Not the biblical kind.

I went to the Talmud, and there I realized that the entire problem, the entire theme of sanctuary, is always linked to war and peace. So what is a sanctuary in the biblical sense? It is an outgrowth of violence. For this reason, we are totally opposed to war, not only war against peoples but also war against individuals. When a state declares war on individuals, that means that something is wrong with that state. Then we have to find another concept of sanctuary.

What is it? Here again I come to my Jewish tradition, and with delight I discover that when we speak of sanctuary in the Jewish tradition, it refers to human beings. Sanctuary, then, is not a place. Sanctuary is a human being. Any human being is a sanctuary. Every human being is the dwelling of God—man or woman or child, Christian or Jewish or Buddhist. Any person, by virtue of being a son or a daughter of humanity, is a living sanctuary whom nobody has the right to invade.

I have seen the opposite. I have seen the invasion of obscurity into light, of violence into wisdom. I saw it forty years ago. Most of you have studied the Bible. As you know, in the Bible forty years make one generation—which means we are one generation away from those times.

I remember *when* I became a refugee. Of all things it was on a Saturday, on the Sabbath. The gathering took place in the synagogue because the enemies, in their perverted imagination, tried so to hurt us that they sought to commit the worst crimes in our holiest place. Therefore they gathered the Jews of my town, Sighet, into the synagogue. And it is there that the first humiliation occurred.

We stood in line; there was a table with many gendarmes, feathers in their hats. We would come and give our papers. We were so naive. We thought that we were protected by our papers. Therefore proudly we took out our citizenship papers certifying us as citizens of Hungary. May I tell you, my good friends, what we had to do in order to obtain those papers? I cannot begin to tell even you. I remember the pain and the anguish that some of us had to go through to prove that our great-great-grandfather was born in a particular village, or town. Finally, we got the papers, and we felt good about them. We felt safe. But then, when I approached the table, in the synagogue courtyard, the officer didn't even look at the papers. He took them, tore them up, and threw them into the wastebasket. I thus became a refugee. That feeling of being a refugee lasted and lasted for many, many years—in fact, until I came to this country.

You who are so-called illegal aliens must know that no human being is "illegal." That is a contradiction in terms. Human beings can be beautiful or more beautiful, can be right or wrong, but illegal? How can a human being be illegal?

I was in France for many years, always as a refugee. Only here did I become a citizen, and I must tell you that I feel nothing but gratitude to this country, the first country that offered me a home and a refuge. I can tell you, my good friends from El Salvador, from Guatemala, and other places, that I hope you will soon feel what I feel. The twentieth century has created so many symbols, so many new concepts. It has also created a new human species: the refugee.

Now what is the characteristic of a refugee? It is that she or he has no citizenship. Hundreds of thousands, if not millions, of human beings have felt— overnight—unwanted. Now nothing can be more painful than being unwanted everywhere, undesired, and this is what a refugee is.

What has been done to the word *refuge*? In the beginning the word sounded beautiful. A *refuge* meant "home." It welcomed you, protected you, gave you warmth and hospitality. Then we added one single phoneme, one letter, *e*, and the positive term *refuge* became *refugee*, connoting something negative.

What I hope this century will achieve before it reaches its end is to get rid of this species. No more refugees. Wherever people come they should be accepted in every society with friendship, they should be given a new way and a new measure of hope by becoming citizens of that country, our brothers and our sisters.

How does one achieve this? I know that American public opinion has political influence. If the American public were made aware—through newspapers and through television—of what is happening, if they were shown the suffering of the refugees, they would move Congress to act.

After all, Congress is our best ally. I am pleased to hear that Senator DeConcini has introduced a bill. I think we should work with all our friends in Congress so that the bill passes in the House and the Senate. I think that is the way we must follow. I think it can be done. It can be done because humanity is contagious. We have seen it.

I'll give you an example. A few months ago I was in St. Louis with my friend Harry Cargas. I spoke for Christians and Jews; it was just a day or two after we heard and saw what was happening in Ethiopia.

Well, we tried to alert people, we spoke, we mobilized sympathies, and the American people responded beautifully. I know that in the places where I was every child in every school gave a dollar. Communities galvanized their strengths, and there too, Jew and non-Jew came together. For it was unbearable to see men and women suffering, dying in front of us. I literally couldn't take it. Nor could the American people.

No comparisons should ever be made between tragedy and tragedy. Every tragedy is *sui generis*. It's only for you—I mean you, victims—to find the name for your tragedy. I have no right to give it a name, but I will accept the name that you give me. The least I can do is to accept your testimony, the testimony of the victims, and give it full credence, because you are both victim of and witness to your own cause.

I believe, therefore, that those men and women who decide to leave a country because they are hungry, because they cannot see their children die, or because they cannot see their parents die of hunger, deserve our respect; they deserve our friendship; and they deserve our support, just as do those who flee the very same country or others for political reasons.

Not to be hungry is part of our human right. How to feed his children is the obsession of every father. When a father cannot feed his children, the humiliation of that father or mother or sister, the torture of that family, is something that we here in America should not be able to tolerate. And we cannot tolerate it. We must speak and we must act as one human being to another. We must show that we care.

A few months ago we had a conference in Washington, which we called Faith in Humankind, a conference of rescuers of Jews during the war. It was devoted to what we called the righteous Gentiles. The idea came to us because I wanted to understand what made some people care and, secondly, why there were so few. We brought seventy-five righteous Gentiles to Washington; we brought scholars and philosophers and moralists, and we met together and we tried to understand what it was.

One of the great surprises for me was to realize that those people who cared—or as we put it, who had the courage to care—were not people of high stature. They were not generals, ministers, university professors, or industrialists. Most of them were simple people who didn't even know that what they were doing was courageous; they didn't even know that their acts were heroic.

They did it because it was the thing to do. And I felt then, woe to our society if to be human becomes a heroic act. Today, the times are different; therefore, please never compare, never. But as long as people suffer, I think there must be other people, and more, who should come to help them.

It doesn't even take that much. A gesture, an invitation to dinner, a smile, a meeting here tonight or a conference, or simply an idea that some young and old people come together for the best and most human cause in the world: to alleviate human suffering and to prevent humiliation.

My good friends, having received your calls and letters, how could I not come to be with you?

I am not sure that I can help you very much. I have no political power. All I have is a way of putting some words together, that's all. I represent my words, but these words come from ancient legends and laws, and after all, those legends and laws are not only mine, they are yours as well. To make you feel better, I will tell you a story: Who was the first refugee? Moses? No. Abraham? No. Adam.

Adam was our grandfather. And Adam was our first refugee. I'll tell you when and how it happened. It had something to do with his wife, but if not with his wife, it had to do with a serpent. The serpent was actually very good, because later, I imagine, the Bible knew that a certain Sigmund Freud would come along. I remember how it happened, we all remember that one day Adam fled; he committed a sin and he fled, at which point God said to him, "*Aifo ata*,"—what beautiful words in the Bible—which means "Where art thou?" Adam, "Where art thou?"

The specific story tells us that one day a great Hassidic master, the founder of the Lubavitch movement, was in jail. He too was a refugee. The warden of the prison came to see him and said to the rabbi, "I know that you know the Bible, maybe you can answer me. In the Bible it's written that God asks Adam, 'Where art thou?' Is it conceivable that God didn't know where Adam was?" And Rabbi Meyer Solomon answered: "God knew, Adam did not."

Do we know where we are? That is, do we know our place in history? Do we know our role in society? I can tell you of my experience and of my learning, again, which I have inherited from centuries of sages and disciples.

My place is measured by yours. In other words, my place under the sun, or in the face of God, or in my own memory, is measured by the distance it has from you. In other words, if I see a person or persons suffer, and the distance between us does not shrink, oh, then, my place is not good, not enviable.

Where am I? I am where you are, and if not, who knows where or whether I am at all?

In conclusion, what is a sanctuary? The sanctuary often is something very small. Not a grandiose gesture, but a small gesture toward alleviating human suffering and preventing humiliation. The sanctuary is a human being. Sanctuary is a dream. And that is why you are here, and that is why I am here. We are here because of one another.

CHAPTER 2

A BRIEF HISTORY OF THE SANCTUARY MOVEMENT
Gary MacEoin

In Burlington, Vermont, 16 November 1984, a jury unanimously acquitted twenty-six citizens of trespass charges. They had admitted refusing to leave Senator Robert Stafford's office. But, they argued, the U.S. government is violating international law in Central America, the President has lied about why he is supporting a covert war in Nicaragua, and they as citizens had exhausted all less confrontational means to get elected officials to correct the situation.

The defendants thus successfully invoked the time-honored though seldom applied "necessary defense" doctrine: a minor law (here, trespassing) yields to a major imperative (prevention of war crimes and of violation of the U.S. Constitution).

The sanctuary movement offers the same rationale for helping Central Americans fleeing persecution in El Salvador and Guatemala to enter the United States and to escape detention and deportation to their homelands by the Immigration and Naturalization Service (INS). Participants insist that the present U.S. administration's treatment of these refugees violates the Geneva and Helsinki Accords, the UN Convention on Refugees, and the U.S. Refugee Act of 1980, and that this lawlessness undermines the fabric of respect for the law that maintains our social order far more than does the technically illegal border crossing.

INS spokespersons pooh-poohed sanctuary for two years as an irrelevant gesture. But, like the Latin American *comunidades de base* ("basic Christian communities"), many of whose members it embraced in their forced exile, the movement spread silently across the land. Consequently, a new tactic emerged in 1984, selective prosecution of leaders in places where conservative jurors were likely to support the administration's claim that Central Americans are sim-

14

ply economic refugees seeking a better life and taking jobs coveted by unemployed American citizens.

The stakes are high, not only for the refugees, but for the sanctuary workers. Anyone convicted faces five years' imprisonment and a $2,000 fine for each alien aided. But if the administration thought that the threat would terrify the activists, it must be sorely disappointed. The first result of two indictments in South Texas and sixteen in Arizona was an enormous volume of front-page publicity from coast to coast. Within days of the announcement of the Arizona indictments, the out-of-state registrations for a previously planned symposium on sanctuary in Tucson, Arizona, tripled to over five hundred. More than a thousand Arizonans joined them in twenty hours of discussion and reflection in a synagogue. Several hundred sanctuary workers stayed on for two further days of planning strategy to expand the movement.

To imagine that indictments would frighten off potential sanctuary supporters reveals a profound misreading of the American way. People of faith in the United States—as generally throughout the world—have always responded to the needs that force themselves on their attention. They do not wait for governments to tell them what to do. They do not let governments stop them from doing what they have decided is dictated by their faith commitment.

How this process develops became clear as far back as 1980, when the previous trickle of refugees from El Salvador swelled to flood proportions all along the United States–Mexican border. To care for their pressing needs, churches quickly organized or adjusted existing structures. The concern became nationwide in July 1980, when a *coyote* (a professional smuggler), having collected his fees, abandoned twenty-six Salvadorans in the Arizona desert. Half of them had died of thirst and heat exposure by the time they were found. A crash program of medical and emotional aid was immediately developed by the churches in Tucson, where the survivors were taken.

In common with most other North Americans, all that most people in Tucson knew about El Salvador at that time was that a few months earlier Archbishop Oscar Romero had been assassinated shortly after making an appeal to the President of the United States to stop sending arms that his government was using to kill its own people. Now they were getting eyewitness accounts from survivors that challenged all their assumptions and preconceptions: official oppression of people who were simply demanding the elementary rights of free speech, freedom of association, a living wage, and a voice in the political system; death squads operating in close collaboration with the government to kill those suspected of seeking to promote peaceful reform; torture and assassination of priests, nuns, Protestant pastors, catechists, and other church workers who supported the just demands of the poor.

It was a traumatic awakening for many, and the trauma was intensified by the bureaucratic response of the Immigration and Naturalization Service (INS). The terrified survivors of the desert ordeal were arrested, and preparations began to ship them back to the tender mercies of the regime of institutionalized injustice from which they had fled. The instinctive response was the only one open to people of faith, a response that in addition resonated with the deepest traditions of the United States. This abomination could not be allowed.

As it happened, the specific problem was quickly solved. The Roman Catholic Diocese of Tucson and Saint Mark's Presbyterian Church came up with bond money to free the refugees while they awaited a decision on their request for political asylum. That was in 1980. Thanks to persistent pursuit of the legal process, which can still be made to work in the United States, even if only at enormous human and financial cost, not a single one of the survivors of that nightmare in the desert has yet been returned to El Salvador.

Something else had also happened. A faith community had been awakened to a shocking reality. It was not a question of just a few people. The refugees fleeing for their lives were arriving in the United States in ever-growing numbers, the Salvadorans soon joined by Guatemalans as ethnocidal terror was unloosed on the Indians of El Quiché and Huehuetenango in that country. And the INS was rounding them up and shipping them back, a thousand or more a month, to what for many was torture and death.

This institutionalized process of injustice obviously called for organized countermeasures. A task force was created by the Tucson Ecumenical Council to harness and direct a response of faith at all levels. That response included a formal proclamation of biblically based motivation: a weekly ecumenical prayer service outside the federal building that houses the INS offices, a service that has now continued without a break for five years. It included the support and expansion of community-based legal services to advise refugees of their rights and help them through the bureaucratic maze. It involved the raising of three-quarters of a million dollars for bonds and legal expenses.

Less dramatically, but no less effectively, other faith communities were summoned to respond in similar ways to the same needs, first near the border from Texas to California, then—as the refugee flood swelled—as far north as Chicago, Boston, New York, and Washington. Gradually networks formed to cooperate in imaginative responses to the challenge: legislative and judicial initiatives, educational programs, shareholder resolutions that, for example, forced all U.S. airlines to refuse to carry Salvadoran refugees back to be killed. By October 1981, the network had developed to the point that delegates from California, Arizona, Texas, and Washington, D.C., met at El Centro, California, to work out common approaches to providing material aid and ministry.

These efforts saved many refugees from deportation. But they did not change either the INS policies or the broader policies of the administration. The governments of El Salvador and Guatemala could and did continue to oppress their citizens and thus create more refugees. In ways that were unethical, immoral, and often illegal (as detailed later in Chapter 13), the INS continued to return thousands of Salvadorans to an uncertain fate: for some, a mercifully quick bullet in the brain; for others, mutilation, rape, and the drawn-out agony of torture.

With the change of administration in Washington in 1981, the situation deteriorated radically. Bail bonds were gradually raised from $100 or $250 to $1,000, $2,500, often $5,000 or more. Those bonded out were denied work permits. In order to survive, they had to join the marginalized work force in sweat shops and restaurant kitchens, where they were underpaid, unorganized, exploited, and denied public assistance, health insurance, and hospitalization.

Following the October 1981 meeting in El Centro, California, a consensus quickly developed among the groups around the country who were involved in supporting and protecting the refugees that the increasingly unethical and immoral practices of the INS demanded a corresponding intensification of appropriate counteraction by the faith community. The concrete form it took was largely determined by one man and his wife.

Jim Corbett, a Quaker with a degree in philosophy from Harvard, had worked for years as a rancher on both sides of the Arizona-Sonora border. He knew not only the two languages but all the characteristics of the terrain.

On 4 May 1981, a friend had given a ride to a young man who turned out, when they were stopped by the Border Patrol at a checkpoint, to be a Salvadoran who had—in INS technical language— "entered without inspection."

The next day, having heard of the incident from his friend, Jim Corbett telephoned the INS and the Border Patrol, only to be told by each that they gave no information about detainees. Surprised and annoyed by this bureaucratic secrecy, he called a high INS official. Speaking with an air of authority, he said he was Jim Corbett and he wanted to know the name and location of a Salvadoran intercepted the previous day at Peck Canyon roadblock. As he had hoped, the official assumed he was another Jim Corbett, a former mayor of Tucson then an official in the Pima County government. Having obtained the Salvadoran's name and location, Corbett consulted with Father Ricardo Elford, one of the group then putting together what was to become the Task Force on Central America of the Tucson Ecumenical Council. Then, armed with a G–28, the form needed to designate a legal representative, Corbett went to the Nogales (Arizona) jail, interviewed the Salvadoran, and had him sign the form. While at the jail, he learned there were several other Salvadorans being held, so he went out for more G–28s. By now, the INS people had realized he was not the Jim Corbett they had thought. When he returned, they asked him to wait, then informed him that all Salvadorans had been moved and refused to disclose where they were.

Corbett was understandably shocked at the discovery that the INS was ready to stoop to such trickery to avoid fulfilling its obligations toward refugees. That reality was further confirmed when a paralegal went to the major INS detention camp at El Centro, California, four hours distant by road and nearly as distant from other sources of appropriate legal advice in California. An INS official took the G–28s she was carrying, tore them up, and tossed them in a trash can. It was a fatal abuse of authority. A court injunction opened up El Centro to the Tucson group, and soon Jim Corbett's two-room converted garage was housing twenty or more Salvadorans bonded out from El Centro to await rulings on their claims for political asylum.

Simultaneously, contacts were being made with Bruce Bowman, a Los Angeles lawyer who (together with Alicia Rivera, a Salvadoran refugee) was putting together El Rescate, a legal aid office to counsel Central American refugees, and with Gus Schultz, a Lutheran pastor (now bishop) in the San Francisco Bay Area. These were the first links in what would grow to be a national network. Gus had pioneered sanctuary for conscientious objectors to the Vietnam War in Berkeley a decade earlier. He was now talking with his weekly clergy reflection group about sanctuary for Central Americans.

When Jim Corbett's two rooms could no longer contain the growing stream of refugees, Jim turned to John Fife, pastor of Southside Presbyterian Church and a member of the steering committee of the TEC Task Force on Central America. In addition to the adobe church, John had a few ramshackle buildings that could be made habitable. By this time Jim was not merely sheltering Central Americans who had been bonded out and were thus "legally" in the country within the INS understanding of the law. While many were organizing, praying, fund-raising, and doing legal work, he had come to a simple yet difficult conclusion. If God was calling the community of faith of Tucson to serve the needs of refugees, the most basic of their needs was to prevent their being intercepted where they were most vulnerable. Capture at the border led to separation of families, humiliation, imprisonment, coercion, deportation, and—all too often—death. So Jim contacted Catholic churches in Mexico where Central Americans were sheltering while they waited for an opportunity to cross over. They now had a skilled coyote—and free of charge.

John Fife sympathized, but as pastor he had commitments. It was for his Session to decide. At its October 1981 meeting he read a statement by Jim Corbett that explained clearly what was involved.

Because the U.S. government takes the position that aiding undocumented Salvadoran and Guatemalan refugees in this country is a felony, we have no middle ground between collaborating and resistance. A maze of strategic dead ends can be averted if we face the imperative nature of this choice without attempting to delude ourselves or others. For those of us who would be faithful in our allegiance to the Kingdom, there is also no way to avoid recognizing that in this case collaboration with the government is a betrayal of our faith, even if it is a passive or even loudly protesting collaboration that merely shuts out the undocumented refugee who is at our door. We can take our stand with the oppressed, or we can take our stand with organized oppression. We can serve the Kingdom, or we can serve the kingdoms of this world—but we cannot do both. Maybe, as the gospel suggests, this choice is perennial and basic, but the presence of undocumented refugees here among us makes the definitive nature of our choice particularly clear and concrete. When the government itself sponsors the crucifixion of entire peoples and then makes it a felony to shelter those seeking refuge, law-abiding protest merely trains us to live with atrocity.[1]

After four hours of prayer and reflection, the Session voted (with two abstentions) to extend the hospitality of the church to the refugees. As they arrived, the ministry broadened. Doctors volunteered their services for malnourished children, for victims of torture. People brought food, were soon inviting refugees to stay in their homes. Some joined Corbett in his work on the border. It was all done in the utmost secrecy, but the INS soon realized that something unusual was happening and sent a message, indirect but clear: "We're not exactly sure what you're up to, but stop it or we'll arrest and indict you."

At about the same time, Jim Corbett was testifying at a National Council of Churches consultation on immigration in Washington, D.C. Speaking of the more than a hundred thousand Salvadorans who had fled their homeland in the previous two years, forced to enter the United States because unable to survive in poverty-stricken Mexico, he said:

[They] are fleeing from military and death-squad violence, from guerrilla violence, and from what might be termed bushwhacker violence; but the situation's generative feature is that their government has instituted a program of systematic terrorism calculated to traumatize the populace into acceptance of established patterns of rule. In much of Latin America, similar programs of military terrorism exist and are being further developed under a unifying U.S. sponsorship that combines massive arms buildups, extensive military training, advanced intelligence technology, regional integration of military forces, and destabilization of governments considered politically incompatible. Consequently, the Salvadorans are probably only the first wave of an influx of Latin American refugees fleeing this military terrorism who will reach the United States through Mexico in this decade.

To save our national soul, Corbett continued, will require a daring and creative response from the faith community, from the church.

The most urgent need of the vast majority of Salvadoran refugees in the United States is to avoid capture. . . .

Much more than the fate of the undocumented refugees depends on the religious community's participation and leadership in helping them avoid capture. If the right to aid fugitives from government-sponsored terror is not upheld in action by the churches—regardless of the cost in terms of imprisoned clergy, punitive fines, and exclusion from government-financed programs—the loss of many other basic rights of conscience will certainly follow.[2]

In the same month, January 1982, the entire congregation of Southside Presbyterian responded to Corbett's challenge and to the challenge of the INS. After five hours of debate, prayer, questions, prayer, reflection, and more prayer, they decided by secret ballot (two negative votes and four abstentions) to "publicly declare Southside Presbyterian Church a sanctuary for refugees from Central America." Other faith communities with which it was in contact, including Gus Schultz's cluster in the Bay Area, also responded. A date was agreed upon: 24 March 1982, second anniversary of the assassination of Archbishop Oscar Romero.

The previous day, John Fife wrote the attorney general of the United States, William French Smith, notifying him that Southside Presbyterian was declaring itself a "sanctuary" for undocumented refugees from Central America and was receiving an undocumented Salvadoran refugee into its care and protection.

We take this action because we believe the current policy and practice of the U.S. government with regard to Central American refugees is illegal and immoral. We believe our government is in violation of the 1980 Refugee Act and international law by continuing to arrest, detain, and forcibly return refugees to the terror, persecution, and murder in El Salvador and Guatemala.

We believe that justice and mercy require that people of conscience actively assert our God-given right to aid anyone fleeing from persecution and murder. The current administration of the United States law prohibits us from sheltering these refugees from Central America. Therefore we believe that administration of the law is immoral as well as illegal.

We beg of you, in the name of God, to do justice and love mercy in the administration of your office. We ask that "extended voluntary departure" be granted to refugees from Central America and that current deportation proceedings against these victims be stopped.

Until such time, we will not cease to extend the sanctuary of the church to undocumented people from Central America. Obedience to God requires this of us all.[3]

Southside Presbyterian thus became the cradle of the loosely structured sanctuary movement, which today encompasses some two hundred churches, ecclesial communities, and synagogues, supported by more than two thousand churches. The simple ceremony was a formal profession of Tucson's ecumenical faith. A masked Salvadoran was welcomed at the doorway by Joanne Welter, then president of the Tucson Ecumenical Council; Pastor John Fife; Rabbi Joseph Weizenbaum of Temple Emanu-El; and members of the TEC Task Force on Central America, including Dr. David Sholin (pastor, Saint Mark's Presbyterian), Rev. David Johnson (pastor, Unitarian Universalist Church), Redemptorist Father Ricardo Elford, Velia Borbon of the Office of Hispanic Affairs of the Catholic diocese of Tucson, Rev. Mike Smith (assistant pastor, Saint Mark's Presbyterian), Rev. Ken Kennon (pastor, Broadway Christian), Margo Cowan and Lupe Castillo of Manzo Area Council, Barbara Elfbrandt of the Pima Friends Meeting, Jim Corbett, Gary MacEoin, and Tim Nonn. An overflow crowd packed the small church, located in a poor Chicano neighborhood in southwest Tucson. It was the second anniversary of Archbishop Romero's assassination, 24 March 1982. While television cameras rolled, INS officers across the street photographed and tape-recorded. Then, as ever, sanctuary was an open faith proclamation, an affirmation of the commitment of the church—its weakness symbolized by this 130-foot by 75-foot adobe building—to defend the needy stranger against the might of the world's most powerful nation.

A similar ceremony was occurring simultaneously at the University Lutheran Chapel, Berkeley, California, where Pastor Gus Schultz was flanked by representatives of Holy Spirit Hall, Newman Center (Berkeley), Trinity United Methodist, Saint Mark's Episcopal, and Saint John's Presbyterian, all of whom would shortly declare their own churches public sanctuaries also. Services were held by Rev. Philip Zwerling at First Unitarian Church, Los Angeles, by Rev. John Steinbruck at Luther Place Memorial, Washington, D.C., and at Community Bible Church, Lawrence, Long Island, New York. Those who sent endorsements included the Episcopal Diocese of Ohio, the Unitarian Universalist Service Committee, Darlington Street Church (Boston), and the Social Justice Commission of the Catholic Archdiocese of San Francisco.

Almost overnight, these initiatives captured the imagination of people all across the United States. They were obviously striking a chord in the folk memory of a people whose ancestors had found sanctuary on the North American continent from religious and political persecution in Europe and who had engraved their gratitude and covenant on the Statue of Liberty: "Give me your tired, your poor, your huddled masses yearning to be free."

Within a year, with the Chicago Religious Task Force acting as coordinator for a very loosely structured network, more than forty-five faith communities declared themselves "public sanctuary sites," with the public endorsement and support of more than six hundred "co-conspiring" congregations and religious organizations. An additional fifty sanctuary organizing committees were active in cities, towns, and rural communities from coast to coast. Reflecting the widespread public concern, the major media had joined the religious press in continuing front-page coverage of the phenomenon.

Questioned by reporters, spokespersons for the INS and the administration professed to be unconcerned about what they described as an insignificant sideshow that had a marginal impact at most on the INS task of protecting the nation's borders and that would disappear when the novelty wore off. Actually, as is now known, the INS and the administration were deeply worried. Lies can stick only as long as those who are lying can hide the truth from those they have deceived and convince them that the liars possess a knowledge of the facts not available to anyone else. The growing exposure of members of churches and synagogues to the reality of government-sponsored oppression, torture, and killing of noncombatants in El Salvador and Guatemala through the eyewitness reports of refugees in public sanctuary was exposing the lies and the liars. The sanctuary movement, a faith response to the need of the stranger in our midst, produced the inescapable result of undermining the U.S. administration's policies in all Central America.

The first public move of the INS occurred in South Texas in February 1984. By that time the number of declared sanctuaries and supporting communities had grown to more than double the figures a year earlier, and the momentum of the movement was clearly accelerating. The Border Patrol intercepted an automobile that was carrying Stacey Lynn Merkt, Roman Catholic Sister Dianne Muhlenkemp, a newspaper reporter, and three Salvadorans who had entered the United States without inspection. The judge would not permit them to present to the jury the defense that they were acting out of and in obedience to religious conviction, and Stacey was convicted of the felony of knowingly transporting an illegal alien, a conviction that is under appeal.

In March 1984, Philip Willis-Conger, a staff member of the Tucson Ecumenical Council's task force on Central America, was charged with a similar offense. That case was dismissed on a technicality. Also in March 1984, Jack Elder, director of a halfway house operated by the Roman Catholic Diocese of Brownsville, Texas, was arrested on the same charge, and in November both he and Stacey Merkt were again charged, this time both with illegal transportation and with conspiracy. At this writing, Elder is serving a six-month sentence. In all these trials, the judge ruled out defenses based on the First Amendment right to free exercise of religion, the linking of sanctuary activity to conditions in El Salvador and U.S. policy in Central America, or the singling out of Elder for prosecution because of his public stand in aiding Salvadoran and Guatemalan refugees.

After these inconclusive skirmishes in Texas, a massive attack was launched (as noted earlier) in January 1985 against the birthplace of the sanctuary movement. A federal grand jury in Phoenix, Arizona, handed down indictments against sixteen persons, including two priests, three nuns, and two of the founders of the movement, John Fife and Jim Corbett. The 71-count indictment included charges of conspiracy, bringing aliens illegally into the United States, transporting illegal aliens, concealing illegal aliens, encouraging the entry of illegal aliens, and unlawful entry. Penalties for each of these charges range from six months in prison and a $500 fine to five years in prison and a $10,000 fine. The indictments also listed twenty-five "unindicted co-conspirators," all of whom were granted immunity and notified they may be called at the trial (scheduled for September 1985) to testify for the prosecution.

One definite result of the administration's offensive against the sanctuary movement has been to bring into the open many supporters who had previously been Nicodemuses in the Gospel story—sympathizers, but in secret because of fear. A significant aspect is the growth of public expression of revulsion at the administration's use of informers to penetrate the movement, and, in particular, to enter churches with concealed recording devices, representing themselves as participants both in worship and in meetings of the church community discussing sanctuary concerns.

Such condemnation of administration tactics is not confined to liberal or progressive elements, or even to persons active in church life. Contrary to administration claims, supporters of sanctuary include representatives of all shades of the political spectrum, including prochoice people and antiabortionists, card-carrying Democrats and Republicans, "yuppies," welfare recipients, blacks, whites, Hispanics, business executives, students, educators, physicians, farmers, feminists. It is a Rainbow Coalition, the dream of Jesse Jackson (who, incidentally, is a strong supporter). A common bond unites these people: a certainty that doing sanctuary is a moral obligation to aid children, women, and men who have fled their homelands in fear for their lives. They are also disturbed by what they see as invasion by the state of an area from which the First Amendment to the Constitution excludes it, an approach to the secret police penetration of the social fabric they had thought of as characteristic of Stalinism but alien to the American way of life.

Open support of the sanctuary movement by mainline religious organizations has also escalated. Many, of course, had endorsed it all along. The 1984 General Assembly of the reunited Presbyterian Church (USA), for example, commended the Presbyterian churches that "at risk to themselves, have declared their churches as places of sanctuary for Salvadoran and Guatemalan refugees, and thus by their actions have chosen to affirm the sanctity of human life over conformity with government policies."[4]

Other national bodies now on record as endorsers of the sanctuary movement include the American Friends Service Committee, Clergy and Laity Concerned, Church of the Brethren General Board, National Assembly of Religious Women, Mennonite Central Committee, National Coalition of American Nuns, United Methodist Board of Church and Society, Unitarian Universalist Service Committee, United Church of Christ Office for Church and Society, Pax Christi, Board of National Ministries of the American Baptist Church (USA), Methodist Federation for Social Action, Commission on Home Ministries of the General Conference Mennonite Church, Immigration and Refugee Service of the Lutheran Council (USA), and the National Federation of Priests' Councils (representing thirty-three thousand Catholic priests). National Bishops of the Lutheran Church of America, the American Lutheran Church, and the Association of Evangelical Lutheran Churches have given their personal support to the movement.

Of particular significance is the increased expression of support by the Catholic community, not only because it is the biggest church body in the United States, but because traditionally it had unquestioningly supported the U.S. administration, especially on foreign policy. Indeed, on the sanctuary issue, the bishops as a group had adopted a hands-off attitude, at least in part because of an analysis made by lawyers for the U.S. Catholic Conference and sent— stamped "secret"—to all bishops. The lawyers explained at length the various laws designed to regulate the entry of aliens into the country. Then without any serious evaluation of the UN Convention on Refugees, the 1948 Geneva Convention on protection of civilians fleeing war zones, or other pertinent national and international law, they stressed the dangers involved in an interpretation of the law by private citizens at variance with the administration's views. The warning did not, however, deter all bishops. Archbishop Raymond Hunthausen of Seattle is one who makes his own decisions, and on this issue his mind has long been clear, as evidenced by the quotation from Archbishop Romero of San Salvador over his desk: "The cry of liberation of these people is a clamor ascending to God that nothing can stop."

In a letter to the people of his archdiocese, Hunthausen wrote: The Immigration and Naturalization Services have chosen to deny these innocent victims refuge. It is my judgment that one of their reasons for doing so is that they find it politically embarrassing to admit that the governments which the United States supports cannot protect their citizens from violence. . . . Some can provide the refugees the means to support themselves. . . . A few will be able to go the last step and offer refugees from Central America sanctuary from the law, which in this case is being applied unjustly. I want you to know that the Archdiocese will support any and all of these efforts on behalf of Central American refugees. . . . I urge you all to join in these activities.[5]

Other bishops who have joined Hunthausen since the administration began to infiltrate the movement and indict its leaders include Bishop Joseph Fiorenza of Galveston-Houston. Stacey Merkt and Jack Elder, he has said, were convicted of "practicing their Christian faith."[6] Bishop John Fitzpatrick of Brownsville, Texas, agrees: "I am proud of Jack and Stacey and those who lay their reputations and lives on the line to protect, nourish, and care for the poor of other nations who seek nothing more than the same opportunity our refugee forefathers sought and obtained during the past two or more centuries."[7] For Archbishop Rembert Weakland of Milwaukee, "Sanctuary is not a way of avoiding justice, but a holy respite so that justice can eventually be done."[8] After the Arizona indictments, Bishops Manuel D. Moreno of Tucson, Thomas J. O'Brien of Phoenix, and Jerome J. Hastrich of Gallup (New Mexico) issued a joint statement: "The persons involved in the sanctuary movement are acting on their moral and religious convictions that the refugees from Central America are victims of political instability, terrorism, and the interplay of regional and international forces beyond their control. Their participation in offering sanctuary is consistent with our national history and biblical values. . . . Their choice represents a moral position, publicly affirmed."[9]

Not less important is the corporate adhesion of major Catholic religious orders. "We the Maryknoll Sisters, Brothers, Fathers, and Lay Missionaries affirm our support for the Sanctuary Movement and for those on trial for transporting Central American refugees," reads a March 1985 statement. "We have lived and worked among the poor of Central America for the past forty years. . . . We know personally some of the refugees. . . . Many of them served their communities as catechists and local church workers. . . . We defend these refugees as 'political refugees' fleeing persecution. . . . The Sanctuary Movement rightfully upholds the 1980 U.S. Refugee Act and the UN Protocol on Refugees. . . . We join the Sanctuary Movement in calling on our government to uphold this tradition and those laws."[10] Also in early 1985, the chapters of the western provinces of the Franciscans (sixty houses) and of the Redemptorists (twenty-three houses) called on each of these houses to proclaim itself a sanctuary.

One conclusion is clear. The administration's assault on the sanctuary movement has both strengthened and expanded it. Because of the movement's decentralized decision making, it cannot be destroyed by chopping off the heads of its leaders. The work goes on as usual even while those indicted are in the dock. It will go on if they are jailed. In this, the movement resembles the Latin American *comunidades de base* ("basic Christian communities"), which sprang up in Brazil in the late 1960s to replace the more formal civic structures crushed by the military dictatorship. They became a network of horizontally related units that maintained the people's morale and finally forced the military to yield in Brazil. Today such units are the infrastructure of the popular resistance in El Salvador.

The comparison with the *comunidades de base* is also appropriate at another level. It was participation in these *comunidades* that brought many previously superficial believers for the first time to a depth of commitment that forced them to respond to their faith's demand that they do justice and struggle for justice. The many North Americans now being directly exposed to, and living with, these refugees are being similarly affected. Personally enriched by the witness of the poor, who, coming out of a condition of hopelessness, retain a spirited, vital flame of faith and hope, they not only are committing themselves to solidarity with their oppressed sisters and brothers but are acquiring a new vision of their role in life. To use a phrase pregnant with meaning in the history of religion in the United States, the sanctuary movement is the Great Awakening of the 1980s.

NOTES

1. John M. Fife, "The Sanctuary Movement," *Church and Society* (March-April 1985): p. 19.
2. "Witness to Immigration," testimony from a consultation sponsored by National Council of Churches in Washington, D.C., 28–30 Jan. 1982.

3. Letter to William French Smith from the Reverend John M. Fife, dated 23 March 1982.
4. Minutes from the 196th General Assembly (New York: Office of the General Assembly, 1984), part 1, p. 335.
5. Pastoral letter issued by Archbishop's Office, Seattle, Washington, 24 January 1983.
6. Tom Morganthau, "No Hiding Place Here," *Newsweek* (4 March 1985): p. 1–4.
7. "Refugee Workers Found Guilty," *National Catholic Register* (10 March 1985).
8. *Catholic Herald*, Milwaukee, Wisconsin (November 1982).
9. Mark Turner, "Bishops Urge Refugee Status for Central Americans," *Arizona Daily Star* (19 January 1985): p. v-1.
10. Maryknoll Missioners, Maryknoll, New York. News release #850206, 24 March 1985.

PART TWO

Theological and Biblical
Perspectives on Sanctuary

CHAPTER 3

HEBRAIC CONCEPTS OF SANCTUARY AND LAW
Davie Napier

My little paperback *Webster's*, although published only a few months ago, does not include "our" understanding of sanctuary. Its two-part definition reads "(1) a sacred place, as a church, temple, or mosque; and (2) a place giving refuge or asylum (such as a game sanctuary)." We know that it is more than a place. We believe sanctuary is a series of related acts, or even only gestures of healing, in a context of incomprehensibly monumental wounds in the corporate body and flesh and mind and spirit of countries and barrios, human communities and families—especially, for us now, in Central America.

Item, from the *New York Times* reporter Raymond Bonner:

The Salvadoran assembly delivered its final blow to the land distribution effort in December 1983. . . . But peasants who lost only a future right to become landowners or were merely evicted from their lands were in some respects fortunate, as the army continued gruesome attacks on cooperatives. A unit of 150 soldiers, for example, raided La Florida, a cooperative 65 miles west of the capital, that was financially supported by the Episcopal Church in the United States and the Anglican Church of Canada. The soldiers seized seven members of the cooperative, hauled them away, tortured and killed them. One man had his nipples cut out. The testicles were slashed off another, the ears of a third. Brains spilled out of one man's head. All had their heads partially or completely severed. None had any bullet wounds. "This is the most horrendous thing I have ever seen in my entire ministry," said the Reverend Luis Serrano, the priest of the 220-member congregation at the cooperative, as he wept. The assassinations left behind widows and 24 orphans. No one was prosecuted.[1]

Those of us who have been listening and reading know that this is commonplace in El Salvador and Guatemala, where it is perpetrated by the military, and in Nicaragua, where the barbaric slaughter is the work of the Contras. All receive training, support, equipment, and dollars from Washington.

We of the sanctuary movement aim to facilitate, in whatever way possible, acts of human healing against the monstrous Central American mayhem that is in pretty full measure at our instigation: U.S. instigation, U.S. manipulation, U.S. intervention. We support small acts, maybe even only gestures, protesting our government's durable, seemingly incurable, national psychosis—the conspiracy syndrome. I do not know where it began in our brief history. A recent writer, commenting on President Polk's seizure of New Mexico in 1846—an act he described as "extending the Union by conquest and preserving it by war"—goes ahead to call that act "the full-blown expression of Manifest Destiny" and the initiation of that familiar twin thrust of so much subsequent U.S. policy: "[To] view history as conspiracy—(in the 1840s the British and the Mexicans were the villains)—then portray U.S. expansion as a just response to fictitious acts of aggression by the conspirators."

The same author, George Black, who is editor of *NACLA (North American Congress on Latin America) Report on the Americas*, comments—in context, not gratuitously: "Jeane Kirkpatrick, that avatar of ideological politics [holds] that Marxism is the enemy, and any action taken to defeat it is moral."[2]

In the second volume of his biography of Eisenhower, Steven E. Ambrose depicts that president as being anticommunist to the point of impeding the quest for peace. Ambrose writes: "He had a penchant for seeing communists wherever a social reform movement or a struggle for national liberation was under way."[3] That essential penchant obtains, alas, for all his successors and is virulently, destructively, and, of course, tragically, operative in this present administration.

Marcionism, the second-century effort to dissociate Hebrew Scripture from the new church, was rightly rejected by the church as heresy. Marcionism, nevertheless, is virulently, destructively, and tragically operative today in the North American religious complex, notably—but by no means exclusively—in what is called the Moral Majority, among whom, to compound the heresy, Greek Scripture (the New Testament) generally exists in a form about as badly mutilated as the bodies of the tens of thousands of victims of the Salvadoran death squads. Not only is the pervasive compassion of Torah lost, but the voice of the prophets is not heard, and even their powerful reaffirmation in the Greek Bible is stifled, distorted, or ignored.

My wife and I were spectators in Jerry Falwell's Thomas Road Baptist Church in Lynchburg in mid-October 1984, and we listened in vain for even a faint echo of thunderous biblical words like *justice*, and its essential synonym *righteousness*. We listened for compassion, interhuman compassion, embodied in the Hebrew word *hesed*; for the kind of interhuman responsibility conveyed in prophetic words quoted by Jesus in Nazareth about ministering to the shattered and the poor and the oppressed. There was no remotest echo of any of these.

It is no wonder that these latter-day Marcionites, these mutilating assassins of Scripture who make up the extensive body of U.S. hardcore fundamentalists, not only voted (apparently almost unanimously) for "four more years," but also gave raucous "Christian" support to U.S. policy in Central America—a policy that quite obviously countenances, instructs in, and pays for indiscriminate torture, rape, mutilation, and murder of innocent folk alleged to be part of a conspiracy, a conspiracy that does not in fact exist, but the fabrication of which justifies monumental slaughter and the continuation of U.S. domination. These fundamentalists view history as conspiracy and then portray U.S. militarism and intervention as a just response to fictitious acts of aggression by the alleged conspirator.

Hear the Hebrew Bible: "Justice is repelled and equity is absent." In the marketplace (one could read: in foreign policy, in economic and political life) integrity is crippled, and the straightforward word is eschewed. "So it is that truth is not here, and anyone who tries to uphold it is cut down."[4]

To name a few in El Salvador that have been cut down: Father Rutilio Grande (March 1977), Archbishop Oscar Arnulfo Romero (24 March 1980), Enrique Alvarez (27 November 1980). Perhaps not entirely coincidentally, Alvarez was murdered just twenty-three days after the election of Ronald Reagan. Nor can we forget Maura Clarke, Jean Donovan, Ita Ford, and Dorothy Kazel, all U.S. churchwomen (2 December 1980). Commenting on this grotesque multiple rape/murder, Jeane Kirkpatrick said: "The nuns were not just nuns. The nuns were also political activists. We ought to be a little more clear about this." And the list could go on and on with all the examples down to the present day. We watch the continued elimination of thousands upon thousands of civilian Salvadorans of all ages and all conditions.

Hear the Hebrew Bible: "Never mind what *they* tell you to do: your peers, the electorate, your governmental prophets and priests. What God requires of you is the doing of justice; the love and the exercise of human compassion; and a stance, surely national as well as personal, that eschews arrogance, imperiousness, and tyranny."[5] All of this is embodied in the prophets' ceaseless cry for justice. The law in its successive major codifications, and clearly under prophetic tutelage, consistently demands particular concern and compassion for the weak, the powerless, and the dispossessed and, perhaps most emphatically, the immigrant, the alien, the sojourner, and the refugee.

And this, of course, is what brings people into sanctuary: our national, corporate, reprehensible responsibility for the creation of conditions that cause refugees to flee here; our knowledge of the law of God; our irrepressible conviction that we must give sanctuary in whatever way we can. Of course we know sanctuary is more than a place; and we remember that three thousand years ago when the state, on the authority of King David, executed the political refugee, David's long-time faithful commander Joab, he was mercilessly cut down and murdered, holding the while in desperation to the very horns of the altar.[6]

The Hebrew term for the alien, the sojourner (who certainly may be the immigrant or the refugee), is *ger*. It repeatedly appears tied immediately to another word, *ezrach* ("home-born, native, indigenous"). There is no suggestion of concern about how and why the *ger* is among us, no interest in differentiation by preresidence background. There is nowhere any suggestion of propriety of presence, that is, "documentation."

In Exodus 12:19, 48–49; in Leviticus 16:29; 17:15; 18:26; 19:34; 24:16; in Numbers 9:14, 15, 29, 30; in Joshua 8:33; and in Ezekiel 47:22 the sense is the same. The alien, the refugee, the immigrant among you, is one of you. There is no distinction. In Exodus 12:49, "The same law shall apply both to the *ezrach* [the native] and to the *ger* [the alien]." In Leviticus 24:22, "There shall be one law for both." In Numbers 15:29, "There shall be one law for both, in the unwitting offense as in the deliberate high-handed act." In a variation, Joshua 8:33 has it in the familiar Hebrew idiom, "Like *ger*, like *ezrach*" (like alien, like native). All Israel equally embraces both.

I suppose no one can determine what "authority" the law of the *ger* may exercise among all of us drawn here under the present meaning of sanctuary. I shall certainly not try. Leviticus 19:34 is certainly one of the ultimate peaks of healing, sensitivity, and compassion in our long-sustained history of interhuman injustice and brutality. The Hebrew says, literally, "Like the native among you shall be to you the *ger*, the *ger* with you [deliberate repetition] whom you shall love." Variations in precise rendering are possible, but not in essential meaning: "whom you shall love as you love yourself."

One would judge, from the persistence and variation of the law's protection and compassion for the *ger*, that the refugee, then in ancient Israel, as now, was an easy object of abuse. The *ger* is singled out in all of the major codes—Covenant, Deuteronomic, Holiness, and Priestly. And in the earliest of these, again literally translated: "A *ger* shall you not oppress; for as for you [plural: 'you-all'], you know the soul [*nephesh*] of a *ger* because you were *gerim* [plural] in the land of Egypt."[7]

There is a profound sense in which we know what it is to be Pharaoh's slaves in Egypt. Indeed, alas, we all know that in Puerto Rico, in Chile, in the Philippines, in the wide world around us, as in Central America, Pharaoh is us, the United States. And of course we know in our own ways the insecurity and humiliation of being refugees and aliens sometimes even in our own land, and maybe particularly in this country at this very time.

Hear now this eloquent statement of the essence of Hebrew law in the tenth chapter of Deuteronomy: "And now, Israel, what does Yahweh, your God, require of you but to walk in the ways of love, to serve Yahweh, your God, with all your heart, . . . [who is] God of

Gods, . . . the great, the mighty, the terrible God, who is not partial and who takes no bribes, [this God it is who] executes justice for the fatherless and the widow, and who loves the *ger*, the refugee."

And hear, finally, God's identification, God's solidarity, with the threatened and hounded. "I have heard their cries and I am come, and I send you, not only to bring my abused people out of Egypt, but permanently to change the blind, stumbling, insensitive imperialist heart of Pharaoh."[8]

NOTES

1. Raymond Bonner, *Weakness and Deceit* (New York: Times Books, 1984), p. 319.
2. George Black, "Unmanifest Destiny," in *The Nation* 239 (20 October 1984): pp. 394, 399 ff.
3. Steven E. Ambrose, quoted by Robert J. Donovan, in a review of *Eisenhower, Vol. II, The President, New York Times* (9 September 1984).
4. Isaiah 59:14, 15.
5. Micah 6:8 (paraphrased).
6. 1 Kings 2:29, ff.
7. Exodus 23:9.
8. Exodus 3:9, ff. (paraphrased).

CHAPTER 4

THE REFUGEE CRISIS, SANCTUARY, AND THE BIBLE
Elsa Tamez

When I think of exile, I turn immediately to Psalm 137, which describes the crisis of the Jewish exile in Babylon. Some experiences—love, joy, pain, exile, death—mark humans deeply in the very essence of their spirit. Such profound experiences remain engraved on our mind, in our heart, perhaps even etched deep in our scarred flesh for the rest of our lives, as moments that will be relived over and over again as circumstances call them back to the surface.

The Salvadoran or Guatemalan refugee is already scarred by such sharp, painful memories—memories of shots, of screams, of tortured, mutilated, quivering bodies of family members butchered in cold blood. These are bitter memories, with overtones of fear, anger, and hate, but also of love and hope. A deep desire to return home accompanies a misery sharpened by the lack of opportunity to earn a living and by the lack of human support or solidarity. There is a sense of profound loneliness and frustration.

We find in the Bible experiences of this kind suffered by the Israelites in their different exiles. A close look at Psalm 137, for example, provides clues to what the refugee suffers, clues that one ought to recognize when expressing solidarity with them. I have chosen a psalm because I think that the poetic language forces us to live intensely the crisis of the poet.

The psalm call us to solidarity with the exile, solidarity that is more than simply providing food, shelter, and other material needs. It is a profound entry into the very world of the exiled refugee and involves feelings often forgotten in our safe, rational world. So we have the ballad of the exile.

"By the streams of Babylon we have sat and wept when we remembered Zion. On the aspens of that land we hung up our harps."

39

For we had been asked to sing to wood cutters, to entertain those who had carried us off. "Sing for us," they said, "the hymns of Zion. How could we sing a song of Yahweh in a foreign land? Jerusalem, Jerusalem, if I forget you, may my right hand wither! May my tongue cleave to my palate if I remember you not, if I place not Jerusalem ahead of my joy. Remember, O Lord, against the children of Edom, the day of Jerusalem, when they said: 'Raze it, raze it down to its foundations!' O daughter of Babylon [i.e., City of Babylon], you destroyer, happy the man who shall repay you the evil you have done us! Happy the man who shall seize and smash your little ones against the rock!"

The allusions in this psalm are to the Babylonian exile. There were altogether four forced migrations during this epoch, starting with the wealthiest Israelites and ending with the poorest. The king was carried off with a number of the royal attendants in the year 605 B.C. Eight years later, the next king was exiled, together with his wife and his mother, 3,000 princesses, 7,100 powerful men, and 1,000 artisans. Next came the turn of the rest of the population, except for a few of the very poor. They were carried into exile in 586 B.C., when Jerusalem was demolished. Finally, five years later, some of the very poorest, who had stayed, joined an uprising against Babylonian rule and were carried off also.

One may deduce from the extremely emotional tone of Psalm 137 that the author must have witnessed the destruction of Jerusalem in 586 B.C. and been one of those then exiled. Consequently, the poet represents the sentiments of the victims of that year, or at least of the final exile five years later.

His experience in exile was one of extreme hardship and suffering, quite different from that of the first group of wealthy people who had been taken to Babylon with the king; many of them eventually opted to stay in Babylon. The poet had a reason to express himself in this particular way. He carries with him the experience of terror.

In the first place, his city was drastically and cruelly reduced to ruins. He saw his people killed, exiled, and forced to flee to other countries. His city, which had been destroyed, was not just any city. It was the Eternal City of Jerusalem, in which it was believed that God resided. The poet, furthermore, was probably an eyewitness of the cruelty of the Chaldeans, who during the invasion did not even spare the children.

In a short poem we are exposed to many deep emotions: nostalgia, humiliation, love, loyalty, courage, bitterness, and hate. The emotions reflect the personal crisis of the author. If we look closely, we can discern five distinct moments.

First comes the experience of sadness and bitterness: "By the streams of Babylon we have sat and wept when we remembered Zion. On the aspens of that land we hung up our harps." Each one of the verbs—to sit, to weep, to remember, to hang up the harp—connotes a break, a sadness. The exile is marked by a bitter memory.

The images—the bank, the river, the aspens—intensify the sadness. And it is not only the poet who wrote the verses who is affected, and not only we who read and share his emotions. For the emotions expressed are not just those of one exile but those of many. "We sat, we cried, we remembered. . . ." What we are looking at here is a community soul. The entire exiled community expresses itself in this bitter poem. In the first verse, the sadness motif appears: the mighty Babylon nearby, the City of Zion far away; the first strange, the second homeland.

The exile doesn't let Babylon's might and greatness deceive him. The Tigris and the Euphrates, with their famous irrigation canals and the aspens on their banks, hold no attraction for these exiles. Their hearts long for little backward Judea. That is why they cry and hang up their harps on the aspens. The verses are nostalgic, and it is not just the nostalgia of voyagers traveling of their own volition. They are the victims of forced displacement. The memory of Zion not only evokes the joys of family and friends, the dear friends, the beautiful places, the worship in the Temple; it includes reliving the nightmare of the invasion of 586 B.C., in which eternal Jerusalem was razed to the ground, her people dispersed.

Next we have the experience of violation and impotence. Our captors call on us to sing for them the lyrics of our songs; our despoilers urge us to be joyous. "Sing for us the songs of Zion," they said. "How could we sing a song of Yahweh in a foreign land?" These verses chronicle the most humiliating memory of their experience in exile, with their captors. It is the violation of their soul. They feel abandoned even by Yahweh, impotent before their oppressors. Such is the sadness of having to live in exile in a strange land, the bitterness of being subject to people who lack all sensitivity for the things most sacred to us. And there is a still further depth to this humiliation. They do not ask for a song, any song. They want a song of Zion. With Jerusalem in ruins, they want to hear the glories of its strength, its eternity, the Yahweh in whom it had placed its trust. The oppressors were not just looking for some folkloric music. They wanted to ridicule the land of Judea, its God, and its people. They wanted to glory in their own power and to demean their victims, victims who at that moment were impotent. The oppressors wanted to rape their very souls, to obligate them for their pleasure, to make them entertain their torturers.

The exiles, nevertheless, refused to sing. To sing a song of Zion in Babylon would imply infidelity to Yahweh and acceptance of their status as captives. Rather than this, they immerse themselves in a deep crisis of faith, struggling to understand the mystery of God.

Finally, the crisis of faith passes. Now we are given the experience of affirmation and promise. "Jerusalem, if I forget you, may my right hand wither! May my tongue cleave to my palate if I remember you not, if I place not Jerusalem ahead of my joy."

The poet changes rhythm here in these verses. The melancholy tone is gone; the humiliation expressed in the first verses has given way to the need for reaffirmation and commitment by the poet to his homeland, his people, his God.

This is an exile who is ready to pay with his life rather than betray his people, culture, and God. He has committed himself not to trade Jerusalem for Babylon as did most of the first Israelites deported. Those who were of royal and powerful status won over the oppressors with their wealth and power; they were able to hold property, to do business, and to prosper in the great city of Babylon. Many had no intention of returning to their homeland, not even when Cyrus of Persia offered all the Jews the opportunity to do so.

Exiles and refugees, especially the poor living in a strange land, feel the need to affirm themselves in order not to lose their identity. These verses let us know that hope exists; the crisis of faith that was seen in the previous verses is past. For through these solemn words the poet opts for frustrated, humiliated Jerusalem.

Perhaps at this point the psalmist realizes that God cannot be demolished like Jerusalem, nor can he overlook injustice. Theology is changing. God is living on the side of the poor, on the side of Jerusalem and its poor and oppressed people.

There is a significant change here. Instead of the first person plural, we have the first person singular. In the first verses we read: "We were sad, we wept." Now we read: "If I forget you, Jerusalem." The promise and the affirmation of identity have to pass also to each individual.

What is striking here is the stress on the word *joy* and the word *happy*. How they contrast with "we wept" and "we hung our harps." In the first verses they were crying in nostalgia and sadness for Zion. Here, on the contrary, they are dedicating themselves to total joy, thinking of Jerusalem. With this attitude of jubilee toward Zion, the exile maintains living hope.

We next move to the experience of resentment and vengeance: "Yahweh, remember against the children of Edom the day of Jerusalem, when they said: 'Raze it, raze it down to its foundations.' " In these verses and the ones that follow, the poet relives the depth of his resentment and bitterness. For the first time he addresses himself directly to God, and his petition is one of resentment.

He begs God to act not only as his defender, but as avenger against the Edomites. The Edomites were the descendants of Esau, brother of Jacob. It had been hoped that they would side with their brother of Judea and not align themselves with Babylon. However, the first captives that they took, they killed, thus becoming traitors to their brothers, the Judeans.

Various parts of the Bible stress this lack of solidarity, this act of treason against Judea. Obadiah, for example, upbraids them for having stood by as the strangers carried off his riches, as barbarians passed through his gate and cast envious looks on Jerusalem.

Remarkable also is the experience of hate and pain: "Babylon, you destroyer, happy the man who shall repay you the evil you have done us! Happy the man who shall seize and smash your little ones against the rock!" Those verses represent the climax of crisis in the exile. The sad, furious poet explodes and lets all the hate accumulated against the oppressor fly from his mouth.

Here all the experiences seen up to this point are united: bitterness, pain, sadness, impotence, vengeance, courage, love, and hate.

The first person plural is used again. Now the whole people express their desire that Babylon should suffer the same damage that Judea suffered, no more and no less.

The poet demands the elimination of the destructive empire. He begs for vengeance like the martyrs of Revelation who cried out from beneath the altar: "How long, O Lord, holy and true, until you judge and avenge our blood on those who dwell on the earth?"

These final verses are indeed horrifying. Readers who have never had such an experience may wish to silence the poet, to distance themselves from the terror and anger of the exiled community. But it is precisely here in the last verse that the crisis of the exile becomes most evident. What it tells us is where the exile has the greatest need for consolation, solidarity, and hope, for it is exactly these images of his own children that keep him from sleeping. This is the end of a poem that has no end. For it is still being sung today in Guatemala and El Salvador.

Response by Philip Wheaton

I want to place the suffering of the Jews in Babylon in a double context. First, it is important that we understand the cause of that exile. According to the exilic prophets, it was Judah in Egypt whoring after the Assyrian and Babylonian empires of the Middle East during the eighth, seventh, and sixth centuries B.C. The word used over and over again in the Old Testament by the prophets is *harlot*. You went whoring after false gods; the leaders, the kings, false prophets, of Israel in the north and Judah in the south sold their birthright in order to gain power and prestige or to save their particular regime. The worship of false gods, that is, idolatry, ended by destroying Israel, the kingdom to the north, and Judah, the kingdom to the south, in 586 B.C.

The warning of Jeremiah to the exiles carried away into captivity in Babylon, had two elements to it. First of all, he said, take advantage of your time in Babylon. In their sharing, the Central American refugees have made clear to us that they are here with a plan, as well as dedication to find a way to go back, to return to their promised land; their plan includes the raising of our consciousness so that we can help them in that task. The other warning of Jeremiah to the

Jews in Babylon was to beware of idolatry, to beware of the worship of false gods and never to forget Zion. This is relevant for our current struggle.

It is important for us to remember that idolatry is our greatest threat. We must beware of the idolatry that we face in this country: the good life here in America, expressed in thousands of ways to us every day. For example, I saw two advertisements recently on television; one said you can have it all, and the other said that life doesn't get any better than this, meaning that you shouldn't look for anything else because here in this consumer society you have all that your heart desires. Beware then, citizens of this empire! Beware of the magnificence of this Babylon, because you stand in danger of being seduced by false gods and worshiping before false altars, the altars of the national security state, the altars of the good life, the altars of those who would lead us down a path of increasing repression in this country. I emphasize that the idol before which we all stand in this country is not a particular person, not a particular administration, but a system of exploitation and repression that is being felt everywhere in the Third World.

I have just come back from the Dominican Republic and Puerto Rico, and I was there reminded of some important facts pertinent to the current situation in Central America. Because of the U.S. invasion of the Dominican Republic in 1965, 800,000 refugees had to flee the Dominican Republic; they now live in the environs of New York City. As a result of the U.S. occupation of the colony we call Puerto Rico, 2.2 million Puerto Ricans have had to migrate to the United States. A. U.S. invasion of Haiti brought to power the late "Papa Doc" Duvalier, the first member of a dynasty that since 1972 has produced an estimated two million refugees—many of whom have come to our country as "boat people." So we are facing a system, not simply an exception to the norm in one country or another in Central America.

My second point is the nature of the idolatry described in the story of Moses descending from Mount Sinai with tablets of stone upon which were engraved: "Thou shalt have no other gods before me." The other god, the other idol before which the children of Israel were dancing and bowing down, was the idol of the golden calf, the worship of mammon. And that is the idol before which our North American system worships at the highest levels of our society—and often at the lowest levels as well, even among us ordinary folk.

It was gold the Spaniards sought when they came to Santo Domingo, Panama, Mexico, and Peru—*El Dorado*, the golden calf. It was the golden juice of the sugar cane that the British sought in the Caribbean islands of Jamaica and Barbados and in the country of Guyana.

Indeed, it was the wealth of the sugar obtained by exploitation of millions of African slaves that produced the excess profits with which Great Britain built its industrial revolution. And it was the golden coffee of Guatemala that first brought the Germans and the bananas that later brought the American corporation called the United Fruit Company. This led the board of directors of that company, under the leadership of John Foster Dulles, then secretary of state, and Allan Dulles, then director of the CIA, to order the invasion of Guatemala by U.S. financed and equipped mercenary troops to overthrow the democratically elected government of Arbenz in 1954.

So before we dump all our disgust and diatribes upon the Reagan administration, which happens at this moment to be attacking the sanctuary movement, let us remember that it was Jimmy Carter, a Democratic president, who ordered the removal of Gen. Humberto Romero from the government of El Salvador in October of 1979 in order to set up a pseudo-agrarian reform attached to a state of siege that resulted in the savage massacre of twenty thousand Salvadorans that year. This in turn led to the massive Salvadoran refugee flow to this country out of which the sanctuary movement has grown. Remember that it was to maintain the linkage of North American corporations with powerful interests in Nicaragua that a Democratic U.S. administration fought against Sandino and his ragtag army between 1927 and 1933, an armed occupation of Nicaragua that brought the death of Sandino and established in power Anastasio Somoza at the order of Franklin Delano Roosevelt, a Democrat, a man who said in 1935: "Yes, he's a bastard, but he's our bastard." That was the United States government. It was also the United States government that blessed the coming to power of Gen. Efraín Ríos Montt, who in 1981–82 carried out the most horrendous slaughter since the time of the Spanish conquest of the Indians of the highlands of El Quiché.

The goal of the Roosevelt and the Carter and the Reagan administrations has been the same: to maintain the dollar high and the peso low, and to sell the poor of Latin America for a pair of shoes. Their goal, to use the words of the prophet Amos, has always been to cheat at the scales, making the *shekel* great and the *ephah* small.

The struggle is not against one man named Ronald Reagan but against an acquisitive economic system based on the law of gain, the maximization of profits, and the degradation of human beings. We struggle against a system whose ultimate concern is not refugees and not dictators and not democracies but the maintenance of an economic order in which we Americans consume most of the wealth and the resources of this planet.

Remember that while we are all concerned about someone pushing the atomic button that could set off an apocalypse, that apocalypse has already occurred for most of the people in the Third World. A theologian of the Disciples of Christ church told me recently in Puerto Rico: "We are not afraid of the atomic bomb; it is for us already the day after." This nation, this empire, is sucking the world dry of its potential resources and land to produce for ourselves, while millions in those lands are starving to death. So, my friends, we are not wrestling against flesh and blood but against principalities and powers in high places, against a system of exploitation.

There are several things we must remember as we welcome the refugees who come here fleeing from terror, from military dictatorships that we all hate. We must remember that they also come here to survive an economic system, in El Salvador and Guatemala specifically, and many other places, with which corporations and the wealthy in this country are in league. We must remember that these U.S. corporations and wealthy individuals make profits off the labor of Salvadoran and Guatemalan peasants, a labor that adds to the wealth of the United States while not leaving the laborers enough to buy rice, beans, and corn.

Let us continue our struggle to house and protect the refugees, as we must do. Let us contribute the funds that will be used to defend those who have been recently arrested, both North Americans and our Central American *compañeros*, as we must do. But while we perform these tasks, let us always keep in mind that after these people have been arrested and released, that long after the Reagan administration has gone by the board, with all of its peculiar mad excesses, mammon will continue to grind down every person it can in its path. Our personal sacrifice to noble causes is, consequently, not enough. A change is required in the fundamental economic priorities of the American system. And, therefore, as we so rightly hold hands with the refugees, we must increasingly share our bread with them, not just across a common table of the Lord's Supper, but as a nation—and as part of a system in which we are unfairly and unjustly taking the wealth of their sweat and using it for our own enjoyment.

The sanctuary movement has not brought the refugees into our midst as a goodwill gesture on our part to help out these poor folk. Rather, I believe this is part of a larger plan that Yahweh has in store for us: not merely to share our good life with them but to remind us of the profound contradiction of our living in the land of plenty as they live in a land of misery. They are here, I believe, to force us to ask questions about our way of life and our economic system that we perhaps have never asked before. They are our *imago Dei*. They are the image of God before us.

Part of our process in this sanctuary movement, like Mordechai before Laban, is not to bow the knee before this system. This means a tremendous wrenching on our part: not to believe in the golden calf, but to look into the faces of these refugees and there to see our *doxa*, our glory. It means to look into the face of Him who laid down his life for us that we would put aside the enthrallments of this world and walk hand in hand as equals down the path of history.

CHAPTER 5

THE BIBLE FROM THE PERSPECTIVE OF THE REFUGEE
John H. Elliott

Religious and moral reflection on the sanctuary movement involves at least three related issues. One is the issue of historical precedents for the sanctuary movement in the Judeo-Christian tradition. Second is our interest in defining the basis of our moral imperative regarding sanctuary. Third is our concern about the theological rationale we give for our position on the sanctuary movement. How is our involvement related to our deepest values and commitments and hopes regarding ourselves and our world? And what role does the Bible play in informing and guiding these values, commitments, and hopes? I have been asked to address the third of these issues.

First, a word about perspectives from which we all read the Bible. I teach the Bible at the University of San Francisco. Though a Lutheran, I teach Roman Catholics, Protestants, Jews, Buddhists, and Muslims, so I have a lot of experience in presenting the Bible to people with different perspectives. As I explain to my students, one understanding of perspective came to me when my kids were very little. I would get down on the floor and play around with them. That was when I began to see what the world looks like from the vantage point of a two- or three-year-old. From a toddler's point of view, all there are are big, round, tall things that we never get to see the tops of, and lots of legs and lots of impediments to where we want to go. Yet, objectively, it was exactly the same world that I saw when I stood up and looked at it from my on-top-of-things perspective.

We read the Bible differently because we bring different perspectives to the reading of the Bible. However, it is not the Bible that is different. It is we who are different. And until we begin to try and understand the Bible from the vantage point and cultural-historical location of the people who wrote it, and for whom it was intended, we will always misread, misapply, and misappropriate the Bible to our own particular circumstances and preoccupations.

The Bible is an inspired and inspiring record of displaced and dispossessed peoples who have found a communal identity and a home with God. As such, it provides an important perspective for reflecting on responsibilities toward refugees and on the significance of the sanctuary movement as a holy action of a holy people empowered by a holy God.

The Bible in an important sense is a book written by refugees for refugees. It was written about a man named Abraham who, along with his family, was called to leave his land and become a sojourner, a resident alien in a foreign land. Abraham is recognized as the father of a pilgrim people. The Jewish people are the people of the Gola, the people of the dispersion, "strangers in a strange land" ever seeking a permanent home. That is a fundamental self-identification of the Jewish people, and inasmuch as Judaism is the parent of Judeo-Christianity, it is a fundamental definition of Judeo-Christians as well.

Since the Bible is a book by and for refugees, they are the people who perhaps best understand it existentially. If we do not see ourselves as refugees, we ought to listen carefully to those who can relate this record of refugeeism to contemporary personal and social experience. Most North American *gringos* do not think of themselves as refugees. Moreover, we are the ones who have caused the current refugeeism. Therefore, we are going to have enormous problems reading the Bible, because it was not written by us, for us, or regarding our circumstances.

Speaking specifically of sanctuary, the word comes from *sanctus*, the Latin translation of the Greek word *hagios*, which itself is a translation of the Hebrew word *kadosh*, the word used in the Hebrew Scriptures for what God is and what the people of God are. "You shall be holy as I, the Lord your God, am holy,"[1] The rabbis regarded that as the central teaching of Torah. In the New Testament it is taken up as the central identification of the Christian community. When, therefore, we talk about sanctuary, we are speaking about holiness, something basic to our identity as Jews and Christians—nothing marginal, nothing peripheral, but the heart of the matter. It is, of course, important to understand that holy does not mean dressing in white clothes, wearing red hats and shoes, and going around sprinkling everything with holy water. "Holy" identifies that which is considered most powerful in a religion or culture. One relates to holiness with a combination of awe and anxiety, fear and fascination. It reminds one of the song of Mary in the musical *Jesus Christ Superstar*: "I don't know how to love him, he scares me so, I love him so." On the one hand, we are always worried about being destroyed by holiness, and on the other hand, we recognize that holiness and access to it are the means of our salvation.

Holiness is like electricity. I am from New York; I grew up in the Bronx, where we have electric trains that run on a third rail. Every child in New York City is taught from the time that he or she can understand anything to never go near the third rail, that you will melt down if you do. Everywhere one finds big signs that warn against going near the electricity, that tell you if you put your finger in an electric socket you will be electrocuted. But, on the other hand, electricity can be harnessed. Electricity can destroy unless you know how to use it; it can also be a means for re-creating your world. The same is true of atomic power. It is destructive, but it can also be used constructively where appropriate. Both of these are analogies of the concept "holy."

Any culture that identifies certain groups, persons, or times as holy is saying about these groups, persons, times, events, and spaces they they are what determines and defines that culture as a people. In other words, holiness is a qualtiy to which we point to define ourselves as a people and to define the ultimate source and symbols of our power. A related aspect of holiness is that it is a means for distinguishing one group from another, the holy from the unholy. For example, in the Book of Leviticus, there is a section called the Holiness Code (chapters 17–26) that was particularly important to the Jews returning from the Babylonian exile. They were refugees concerned with maintaining a distinctive identity and social cohesion. The Holiness Code was formulated to state who they were and what they were to do as the people of God. The prologue to this code reads:

And the Lord said to Moses: "Say to the people of Israel, I am the Lord your God. According to the doings of the land of Egypt, where you dwelt, you shall not do; and according to the doings of the land of Canaan, where I am bringing you, you shall not do; nor shall you walk in their ordinances. You shall observe my judgments and keep my statutes, to walk in them. I am the Lord your God. You shall therefore keep my statutes and my judgments, which if a man does, he shall live by them. I am the Lord."[2]

A holy people is called to a holy and distinctive way of life by a holy and "wholly other" God. Christianity saw itself as the continuation of the holy people of God and asserted itself over against the Roman Empire.

Like every colonial power, Rome sought to control its subjects through military force and economic exploitation. Christianity emerged in a land staggering under colonial oppression. Its founder Jesus offered to the countless displaced and dispossessed of Palestine a vision of God's power and mercy and an experience of a new form of human solidarity in the family of God. In him, his followers saw the power of God, power no longer vested in a holy building, the temple, but embodied in flesh and blood. The power of his death on behalf of the powerless created a holy, powerful community. Sanctuary was no longer a holy place or a holy temple but a holy community energized by a Holy Spirit and marked by a holy way of life. This holy community drew a clear line between respect for Caesar and trust in God. Its distinctive style of life was characterized by obedience to God's will, faith in God's Messiah, Jesus, and care for the strangers, the naked, the homeless.[3] Christians were to "be holy as the God who called them was holy."[4]

Another function or characteristic of holiness is that it is "contagious." All cultures believe that if you get too close to what is holy, you are going to "catch" it. It is like a contagious disease, so you have to quarantine holy people. That is why we want to know when the holy times of the year are, the holy days. We want to know who the holy people are. You have to put collars around their necks and put them in certain kinds of dress. They must behave in a certain way with certain uniforms, because if you get too close to those people you are going to be "zapped" by holiness. Watch sometime the way people come into synagogues and churches, filling up the back first. If you are unlucky and you get there last, you get seated way up in front, close to where holiness is.

Look, for example, at how the present Bishop of Rome is concerned about getting his people back into collars and habits to identify where the holy people are. We could look at that negatively, but we can also view it positively. Both the Hebrew people and the early Christians believed that as a holy people they could exude holiness just like Typhoid Mary could transmit typhoid. Holiness is contagious. Early Christians did not baptize their children because the children "caught" the holiness of their baptized parents. If holiness is contagious and can be caught, and if sanctuary is the means for creating a space and a time of holiness, it means that by creating sanctuary, being sanctified people, and doing sanctuary, we can actually get other people to "catch" it.

The best example I know is from my own experience in Berkeley, California. Berkeley, of course, is not the experience of everybody, and it is not necessarily typical. But it can happen anywhere. The City Council of Berkeley made a statement that reads as follows:

First, whereas a number of refugees asked that sanctuaries be established, and whereas the University Lutheran Chapel at Berkeley [my church in Berkeley], with the support of the Bay Area churches, has announced its availability as a place of sanctuary for any person who is unwilling to participate in certain actions, and has issued a statement indicating the nature of the sanctuary offered.

Second, therefore, the City of Berkeley supports these people who decide to take sanctuary and the City of Berkeley supports the sanctuary already established at the University Lutheran Chapel and will support any congregation in Berkeley which engages in sanctuary.

Third, the City of Berkeley is also willing to provide a facility for sanctuary. The nature of that sanctuary will be defined by a statement of the University Lutheran Chapel and its supporting churches. A committee designated by the University Lutheran Chapel and supporting churches will work with the City to find an appropriate facility and operate that facility in line with the sanctuary statement.

Fourth, the City of Berkeley encourages the people of Berkeley to work with the existing sanctuary to provide bedding, food, medical aid, legal help and friendship that they may need.

Fifth, no Berkeley city employee will violate the established sanctuaries. This involves the police department, by assisting in the investigation, public or clandestine, or engaging in or assisting arrests for violation of federal laws relating to service on the premises offering sanctuary, or refusing established public service.

This resolution was passed on 10 November 1971. At that time, as you remember, there was a war going on called the Vietnam War of Liberation. And there were men from the aircraft carrier the *Coral Sea*, stationed in the area who, as conscientious objectors, refused to return on the carrier to Vietnam and sought sanctuary. Our University Lutheran Chapel, after careful reflection on our responsibilities, voted to offer these sailors the sanctuary of our church. Little did we know at the time of our decision that what began as the conscientious act of one Christian congregation would soon "infect" an entire city. But so it is with acts of holy contagion. Now, over a decade later, sanctuaries across the country once again are putting to the test the power of sanctuary and demonstrating the vitality of holy solidarity.

NOTES

1. Leviticus 19:2.
2. Leviticus 18:1–5.
3. Matthew 25:31–46.
4. 1 Peter 1:14–16.

CHAPTER 6

BIBLICAL CONCEPTS OF IDOLATRY

Robert McAfee Brown

The recent indictments of sanctuary workers have added a strenuous urgency to the conflict between religion and state. They have also provided a vivid example of biblical concepts of idolatry. There is now a clear conflict between our government and those who give sanctuary or participate in other ways in the movement. We also know that there are informers, members of the FBI, or other branches of our government, who participate in the sanctuary movement, not because of sympathy with our concerns and the plight of the political refugees we are trying to help, but solely and explicitly to betray all of us and the refugees.

Our government now acts to intimidate, to frighten, to spy on and destroy, if it can, the humane concern that we are trying to express. It is, however, fighting a losing battle. Maybe it is a good educational experience for us that we now have a tiny inkling of the first steps of what it is like to live under repressive governments in El Salvador, Guatemala, the Philippines, Chile, Soviet Russia, or, to employ an analogy that is increasingly important to those of us born in the 1920s or before, the Germany of the 1930s.

When a stranger comes up to you smiling, asks your opinion about sanctuary and about lawbreaking in the name of conscience and displays great interest in what your local church is doing specifically and in who some of the people are who are involved, think before you answer. This may be someone whom your tax dollars are helping to support and who plays the role of hypocrite, wearing a mask and representing himself (or herself) as the opposite of what he (or she) truly is. Our government has now adopted a favorite device of totalitarian nations. It pretends to be sympathetic, while infiltrating, ingratiating, and associating. If you are not careful, you can put those with whom you are associating behind bars.

I hope some of those informers will feel twinges of conscience as they realize that obeying government orders forces them to become betrayers of other human beings. To them, I say: "When you tell lies in the service of what your government tells you is truth, you have already betrayed the truth. And you need not do it." Informers can still say no to this destruction of the integrity of their lives, just as some of the rest of us are saying no to the destruction of the lives of our sisters and brothers in Central America.

Why is there a conflict between religion and the state? The answer to that question is contained in the theme to which I address myself, biblical concepts of idolatry. The issue is not new. It is as old as human history, it is imbedded in the biblical story, and it is as fresh as the morning newspaper or the evening news on television. The issue is idolatry: the worship of idols, or false gods. The issue is, Which God will we acknowledge, the true God or a phony god, a fake god, a god of our own construction? In theological terms the issue is not atheism but polytheism. It is not an absence of God in our public life but a proliferation of gods, a whole marketplace full of gods.

And if we define God as that one to whom we give our ultimate allegiance, the one who commands our final loyalty when the chips are down, then the conflict today is clear. On the one side is the God to whom we are trying to give allegiance, the God who sides with the poor and the dispossessed, the God who is the God of justice and compassion, the God who bids us likewise to align ourselves with the victims rather than the victimizers, the God of the Hebrew and Christian Scriptures. On the other is the god of those who infiltrate into our midst to seek our arrest and imprisonment, the god of the state.

The god of the state is the most pervasively worshiped god in the world today. We have an administration and a newly burgeoning group of right-wing Christian think tank professionals who insist that it is the Russians who worship the god of the state. Admittedly, that is largely true, but let us also note how terribly easy it is to say. I am staggered by the ease with which these people can blind themselves to the fact that the worship of the god of the state is becoming more and more widespread in our own nation as well.

We are now being told not to oppose what the state is doing and being warned that if we do not give uncritical allegiance to the state, it will "get" us. During these last few years in El Salvador, when over forty thousand civilians have been murdered by a Salvadoran government that our own government has kept in power, our administration has routinely affirmed every six months that the Salvadoran government was making good progress in extending human rights. This affirmation made it possible for our government to continue to send more arms to their government so that their government could continue to murder its civilians. And when Salvadorans flee from such terror and seek asylum within our borders, our government routinely ships them back, claiming, again routinely, that they are simply looking for bigger and better bucks. They are not political refugees, the State Department tells us, only economic refugees.

This is an act of calculated callousness on the part of our government that, as we all know, exposes the refugees to being murdered. And when, in the name of all that is decent and humane, U.S. citizens say no to this activity of our government and try to counter it, they are spied upon, informed upon, rounded up, indicted, and called to face trial.

It may be, as the Bible says, a fearful thing to fall into the hands of the living God. It is also a fearful thing to fall into the hands of a false god, an idol, a human construct, telling us: "Don't cross my will, don't defy me, don't disagree, for if you do, I will find ways to get rid of you and to get rid of the people you are trying so mistakenly to help."

And so our question becomes very simply, "Which God do we serve, the living God or an idol, the God of the Bible or the god of the state?" I offer two biblical examples of this theme of the false gods, the idols, and the kind of worship they demand. One is taken from the Hebrew Scriptures and one from the Christian Scriptures. They both make the same point, and we can unite Jews and Christians around the theme they represent even as we continue to use our own vocabularies and different ways of spelling out our allegiance to the God we both serve.

In the Hebrew Scriptures, the first commandment, the basic call for allegiance, is found in that familiar story of the people at the foot of Mount Sinai when Moses comes down from an encounter with God and tells them what God asks: "I am the Lord your God, who brought you out of the land of Egypt, out of the house of bondage; you shall have no other gods before me." That is the basic biblical message. The God who sides with the poor, the oppressed, the God defined as the one who brings the slaves out of the house of bondage and oppression, is the God who claims our allegiance and demands preeminence in our lives.

The gods of Egypt, the symbol of ultimate power in the culture of that time, are to be repudiated just as Pharaoh, the head of the Egyptian national security state, is to be repudiated. Later on there are other false gods the Jews have to confront, gods likewise demanding unquestioned allegiance—the baals, the fertility gods of Canaan, the gods of Assyria, Greece, Rome, the Holy Roman Empire, czarist Russia, Fascist Italy, Nazi Germany, Soviet Russia, Franco's Spain, Pinochet's Chile, Idi Amin's Uganda, Marcos's Philippines, and—let us say it—Reagan's America. For whenever Reagan's America claims, as it is claiming on the sanctuary issue, the right to destroy the lives of Salvadorans and Guatemalans by shipping them home to firing squads and the right to destroy the souls of North Americans by denying them the right to grant sanctuary to victims of oppression, we have the same kind of idolatry at work. "You shall have no other gods before me," says the God both Jews and Christians worship, especially not a government god that begins to take on the trappings of the national security state by saying it will make the decisions about who can live and die, who can protect whom, who shall be allowed to go free and who shall be intimidated, indicted, and incarcerated.

The same message, "You shall have no other gods before me," is also contained in my example from the Christian Scriptures, where idolatry is once again repudiated, this time in the language of Christian symbolism.

In the early church the most basic Christian confession of faith was only two words long. As a theologian who has had a professional obligation to wade through endlessly long creeds and confessions, I have often wished that subsequent Catholics and Lutherans and Talmudists had been as economical as their forebears were in their use of words. This confession went: *Kurios Christos*, meaning Christ is *Kurios* or Lord. *Kurios* is the Greek for that to which or to whom ultimate allegiance is given. "Who is your *Kurios*?" early Christians would be asked. The response for them was clear, "the *Christos*, Jesus of Nazareth." It is a response that at first sounds like a purely theological argument, able to engender heated discussion about such things as the relative merits of a docetism or modalistic monarchianism as well as a cause of endless, painful controversy between Christians and Jews.

Let us remember, however, that it was a political statement as well. In the Roman Empire at that time every citizen had annually to make a public declaration of allegiance to the empire. The declaration went "*Kurios Caesar*," meaning Caesar, the state, is *kurios*, is lord. The state is the one to whom I give my ultimate allegiance. So if, instead, you were so rash as to make the theological statement "*Kurios Christos*," Christ is the object of ultimate allegiance, you were becoming very political indeed. You were announcing not only your primary and ultimate loyalty to Christos, but, at best, only secondary and subordinate loyalty to Caesar. Since Christ is Lord, you were saying, Caesar is not lord, Caesar is a false pretender to the title of lord. To affirm Caesar as lord would be to affirm allegiance to a false god, an idol.

Caesars don't like that one bit, whether they reside in Rome or in Washington. So the first commandment and the earliest Christian confession are making the same claim in different language, a claim around which all of us not only can, but must, rally. In the name of saying yes to what is ultimate for us, we must be prepared to say no to whatever falsely claims that place of ultimacy. To say yes to the true God is to say no to the idols, whoever and wherever they are.

The voice of that idol is today the voice of the contemporary Caesar, our own government, which is telling us: "We decree that you must turn your backs on refugees, those who are fleeing from the modern Pharaohs in their own lands. We decree that you grant them no sanctuary, allow them no place to lay their heads, return them to firing squads." If we ask why, they have an answer. "We have decided that they are not wanted here. We have decided in advance that their claims are spurious. We have decided that they are only trying to take advantage of us. Besides, if we granted them refuge, we would be conceding that their government, which we support, is an evil government, and that we cannot afford to do. So, act in accord with us, or we will make it mighty tough for you." Our government has decreed that we who feel strongly about the need to provide sanctuary shall not be allowed to provide it. Our consciences are to be made hostage to repressive measures, against suffering people, by our own government. And we really have no choice but to say no to all of that.

There are people in the sanctuary movement who have said that no so clearly and consistently for so long and have acted upon it so vigorously that they have been indicted and will put up with months of hassle and legal fees and court costs and then possible imprisonment.

They have said no, and they are already beginning to pay the price. If the rest of us really take seriously the biblical call to oppose idolatry wherever it breaks out—especially when it breaks out close to home—we have no choice but single-mindedly to stand with them and give them our very public help and support. To the degree that they are impeded from carrying on the work they have begun, we must take their places and continue their work. We must ensure that what they have been about becomes what we continue to be about.

There is nothing our government would like better than to have that agenda fail, to have us become fearful or divided or to start dissipating our energies in a dozen contradictory directions. To the degree that we allow ourselves to be intimidated by this action of the government, we too will be worshiping false gods; we too will be succumbing to the wiles of the modern Pharaoh, the contemporary Caesar, who this time—let it be clear—resides in Washington.

Let us remember the frightening analogue to what we are confronting today, the rise not so long ago of the Nazi state and its increasingly persistent attempt to get rid of the Jews. If we had been in Germany in the 1930s and Jews had come to us and asked to be hidden because otherwise they might die at the hands of a hostile government, we would all like to think we would have helped them. The fact is, of course, that Christians had an abysmal record in that situation. With a very few brilliant exceptions, everybody caved in, and the state was able to carry out its policies with little resistance.

Translate the question from the 1930s to our own time. If we are Americans in the 1980s and Salvadorans and Guatemalans come to us and ask to be hidden because otherwise they might die at the hands of a hostile government, will we take them in? To the degree that people in Germany failed to give sanctuary and hiding to Jews, to that degree the power of the Nazi government increased and became more repressive. To the degree that people in the United States fail to give sanctuary and housing to Salvadorans and Guatemalans, knuckling under to the tactics now being displayed by our government, to that degree the power of our government to become increasingly repressive will be enhanced and the lives of Salvadorans and Guatemalans even further jeopardized.

We Christians failed the Jews in the 1930s, and we have unfinished business with the Jewish community on that score. But let us at least salvage out of that tragic failure a determination that we will not fail Salvadorans and Guatemalans in the 1980s. The responsibility is inescapable.

Yes, there is a conflict between religion and the state today. Yes, idolatry in the biblical sense is alive and well, flourishing in our midst. To those realities there can be only one response. We must expand our efforts on behalf of the victims, lest, by failing to do so, we betray the victims and become accomplices in the work of the victimizers.

CHAPTER 7

A THEOLOGY OF SANCTUARY FROM A CALVINIST PERSPECTIVE

Richard Shaull

At the beginning of her study of the origins of totalitarianism,[1] Hannah Arendt remarks that one relatively small event, the extermination of the Jews, brought into focus and exposed the process of disintegration of the Western world and the horrendous human suffering accompanying it, the suffering of millions of rightsless people, political refugees inside and outside the countries of Europe who had lost everything necessary for human existence. They lost their homes, which meant the loss of the entire social structure into which they had been born, a structure that established their place in the world. They lost the protection provided by the law, police, and government. They lost any possibility of human community.

Men and women were subjected to accusations of revolutionary or counterrevolutionary activites that not even their accusers believed. They were criminals without a crime, human beings reduced to the condition of savages, victims of the mad ambition of men who no longer were guided by reason and who disdained the whole structure of reality. And in the case of the Jews, at least, before the Nazis set the gas chambers in motion, they carefully tested the ground and found out that no country would claim those people.

As I reread Arendt's account, I was struck by the parallels between the tragic situation of the rightsless people in Europe a generation or two ago and that of the rightsless people in our midst here and now. How better to describe them than as people without a home and without any possibility of finding one? Deprived of any protection of law or government in their own country, they are treated here as criminals, although they have committed no crime. Innocent people are being eliminated by uniformed men, death squads, and bombs in El Salvador and Guatemala. Those who flee this repression are hunted as they wander from one hostile land to another, and when they arrive here, they are exposed to the danger of being sent back to the horrors in their own land that drove them to try to escape in the first place.

Can it be that the tragedy and suffering that we see in the refugees in our midst exposes the irrationality and inhumanity accompanying the disintegration of our American society in the same way that the suffering of the Jews exposed the inhumanity of Europe fifty years ago? In both instances the sensitive Christian conscience faced by such barbarity responded in the only way possible. It took upon itself the defense of the defenseless, surrounding those with no protection whatsoever with the support of a community of sympathy and friendship, countering the destructive madness of the world with the grace of love.

The question raised for the Germans then and for us today is not what to do in these circumstances; it is, rather, whether or not we have the vitality of faith necessary to do what we know is right. In Germany, that response came primarily from small groups of Christians whose lives had been touched by a powerful movement of ideological renewal. The faith that had been eroded by its surrender to modernity was revitalized. The Bible came alive, and men and women were once again confronted by a God present in the world in Jesus Christ who laid a claim upon them from which they could not escape. In 1934, a small group of them gathered in Barmen and made a stirring confession of faith in Jesus Christ as "the one Word of God which we have to hear and which we have to obey and trust, in life and in death." The confessing church was able to maintain a compelling witness through difficult times.

Today, another movement of spiritual renewal is starting, especially in the churches of Central and South America. Its power lies in another mystery discovered in the gospel, namely, that this same Jesus Christ meets us in our poor, suffering, and despised sisters and brothers. What you and I do to the least of them we do to Jesus Christ himself. It is this new experience of Christ by the poor and marginalized, and of his presence in their midst, that has begun a new reformation in Latin America.

The sanctuary movement is part of this movement of spiritual renewal. It is the response of the Christian conscience in our situation to the presence of Jesus Christ in the poor. As such, it is a fundamentally religious movement. With this foundation, those involved in it hardly need theologians to provide a rationale for their stance. In the same way that Jesus Christ laid an absolute claim upon German Christians in the confessing church, this same Christ meets us in the refugee and lays upon us the same claim.

The confessing Christians were patriotic and law-abiding citizens. However, they came to realize that they could serve the interests of their own nation only as they gave obedience to God over any human authority. This meant to stand on the side of defenseless human beings and take up their cause against any power that was threatening them, even though that meant confronting the state itself. Moreover, a religion based on Jesus Christ, who was himself killed by the representatives of law, order, and civilization, constantly needs to question the claims of those in positions of power about the rightness of their cause. It needs to be especially sensitive to every violation of the rights of the poor and powerless, whatever the rationale used to justify it.

Many theologians have spelled out the implications of this across the centuries. Here, I mention one: John Calvin. We often credit him with having established categorically the obligation of believers in Christ to "obey God rather than men." By doing this, he provided the basis for resistance to tyranny on the part of reformed Christians. A closer look at his thought, however, is necessary to appreciate the surprising things that this theologian of order has to say. Reading recently his commentary on Psalm 82, I found this declaration: "Rulers are appointed primarily to be defenders of such as are in misery and oppressed, because they are the ones who stand in need of others' help." Rulers exist in God's providence "to give to the miserable and the oppressed their rights." But in point of fact, rulers are "more inclined to be infatuated with their own greatness, lord over others, and pay greater deference to the wicked and powerful than to the poor and innocent." And when this happens, their order is "established disorder," and those who are obedient to God must be primarily concerned about the restoration of God's order.

If a vital faith and sensitive conscience clearly tell us what to do, what need is there for theologians? I see it this way: When we take to heart the plight of Central American refugees, we very soon discover that we have embarked on a difficult, perhaps unexpected, journey on which we move deeper and deeper into awareness both of the power of evil in our world and the riches of grace. Each step confronts us with new challenges, new dangers, and new opportunities. The theological task before us is to seek—as we stand with the defenseless and pay the price—our reflection from the context of our faith. This can lead us to see new visions, probe new depths of evil, and experience new dimensions of grace. I suggest that there are three ways in which this will happen. First of all, when we become aware of the horrendous suffering of millions of Central Americans in our so-called backyard, when we become aware of the mistreatment of refugees within our borders and realize that those who respond to their cry could be sentenced to long terms in prison, the inevitable question we ask is, What kind of society are we living in that does this?

Certainly if any of our political leaders, from Ronald Reagan on down, were face to face with an abandoned refugee child, they would know what to do and would respond sympathetically. They would also acknowledge the need to assist those caring for such a child. How then can we make sense of the radical difference in response that we see between the sanctuary movement and the administration? Experiences of this sort, I believe, compel us to take much more seriously the systemic character of evil. They help also to understand how our present system operates and how it can do violence to human beings. We live with an economic order dedicated to the pursuit of profits, not to serving the well-being of human beings. It engenders a large-scale bureaucracy that puts a great distance between those who make the decisions and those who are affected by them. This tends to turn people into objects and to allow them to be treated as cases. It produces a society that functions within clear patterns of domination and that is constantly committed, above all else, to maintaining the power of some over others.

Now if we, facing what is happening to refugees, probe the question of systemic evil, I believe we are also prepared to understand the New Testament better, to see what it says about the rule of principalities and powers, the spirit of institutions, as Walter Wink calls it, and how they work. We are similarly better prepared to grasp what the New Testament has to say about Christ's victory over the powers, and what it means for us to live by grace in the midst of our powerlessness as the agents of the power of God.

Secondly, we ask, How can a government that claims to be guided by Judeo-Christian principles, an administration headed by men and women who proclaim themselves for the most part as confirmed Christian believers, some of them "born-again" Christians, launch such an attack against a few defenseless church people? Here we must take our cue from the ideology of national security as it has been worked out in Latin American countries. We have here a logic that, if followed seriously, leads directly to repression and possibly toward totalitarianism. The more critical our national situation becomes, the deeper the crisis of our social and economic system, as well as of our system of values, the more desperate the attempt to shore it all up by presenting it as unchangeable. This we do by claiming that we are engaged in a life-and-death struggle against absolute evil, communism. To survive the attacks of this enemy it is essential that we see our way of life—as absolute good—being threatened by absolute evil.

When we arrive at this point in the development of this ideology, religion is called upon to play a central role, that of defending those values' divine character. Consequently, it is of the utmost importance to the ideologues of national security to have religious groups who play this role, even though in doing so they lose more and more of their Christian essence. In this situation, when a religious movement arises with a total commitment to the poor and the cause of justice and incarnates a radically different form of Christian faith and life, the way is set for open confrontation and irreconcilable conflict. For nothing is more likely to expose the game being played by the misuse of religious symbols and of the church than the simple witness and suffering of those who dare to reveal the presence of God in their lives, their identification with the dispossessed.

There are traps in claiming to be "biblically correct." Any time we begin to speak and act out of conscience based upon religious faith, we are tempted to claim more for it than we should. We are also tempted, especially under great stress and insecurity, to transform our God into an idol, to make our faith into some sort of absolute that guarantees what we already believe.

In the Bible there is a very fine line between the worship of God and idolatry, and every committed Christian has to struggle constantly with that issue. The Christian right has succumbed to the temptation to idolatry. On the other hand, women and men of faith are discovering that they don't need absolutes to sustain them, as their God frees them to live in the midst of insecurity through trust and through grace. The real test of Christian faithfulness is our capacity to draw on the resources of our own faith and discover in doing so what the grace of Jesus Christ is all about.

In this struggle, it is of utmost importance to realize that those who move in the world of false absolutes are not likely to have their reason intact. In fact, as Hannah Arendt reminds us, we only grasp the radical nature of evil when we realize that it is ultimately irrational, that the conclusions reached cannot proceed from motives comprehensible to human beings. The struggle toward which we are moving in our society may well be a struggle with irrational forces of evil. Its challenge can only be met with the simple truth of the gospel lived out confidently in the midst of suffering.

Finally, I believe we must face a third question: Why is it that those who stand with the poorest and defend their interests are being so attacked at this time? This issue is one of reading correctly the signs of the times, of perceiving where the pressures of the coming Kingdom of God are being felt in our time and place. According to the Magnificat, a coming into history of a Messiah will bring down the powerful while raising up the powerless, will send the rich away empty while giving food to the hungry. If Jesus Christ is the Messiah, then his presence in history carries forward this process, and the real battle goes on at each moment in history when a new stage emerges of raising up the poor and breaking the structures of the powerful.

That is precisely what is happening in our time in Central and South America. There we see dramatic signs of the imminence of the Kingdom of God as the poorest of the poor discover their worth in God's eyes and become protagonists of history. As never before, the foundations of power and privilege in Latin America and in the

United States are being challenged. This new manifestation of the presence and power of Jesus, the Messiah, is shaking up the nations of Central America, and it is a process in which Christians are dynamically involved. It is here, also, that the persecution of Christians is and will be the most intense. Once again are the poor themselves persecuted, and with them is the church that stands by their side.

Where does all this leave us? Though it does not provide a neatly worked out theological scheme, I believe it presents us with some clearly defined theological tasks. The first of these is to participate in a process of reflection within the struggle. As we are confronted day to day by new realities we must reflect on them in the light of our faith and, simultaneously, explore new dimensions of human relationships as we receive the gift of life in a new community of faith.

NOTES

1. Hannah Arendt, *The Origins of Totalitarianism* (New York: Harcourt Brace, 1951), p. 1 ff.

Response by Renny Golden

One of the tasks Richard Shaull stressed is that of confronting systemic evil. He said it becomes an ideology of national security that can lead toward totalitarianism. When we think of national security states in Latin America we should begin to measure where we stand in relation to such systemic evils and their ideological manifestations. A good starting place is the Banzer plan (named for Col. Hugo Banzer, who became president of Bolivia in 1971), which is still effectively used against the church in El Salvador and Guatemala today. It was devised by the CIA, and it is significant that its basic strategy continues to determine U.S. policy both in Latin America and here at home. Let us look at some of its major guidelines.

The national security state, it says, never attacks the church as an institution, and still less the bishops as a group. Instead, its approach is to isolate and attack the most progressive church elements and to control certain religious orders. The CIA can be counted on to cooperate in such projects, providing information about certain priests (personal documents, studies, friends, addresses, publications, foreign contacts), for example.

Arrests should be made with minimum visibility—in the countryside, on deserted streets, or late at night. Plant subversive material in the briefcase of a priest who has been arrested, also, if possible, a weapon—preferably a high-caliber pistol—in his room or home, as well as more subversive material. Develop a story to disgrace him with his bishop and the public. Use all available communications media to publish loose, daring, compromising material calculated to discredit progressive priests and church workers. Maintain cordial relations with some bishops and church members, thus assuring public opinion that only a few dissidents, not the church as such, are under suspicion.

This policy, as it is being applied to the sanctuary movement here and now in the United States, forces us to ask ourselves challenging questions: Do we have the vitality of faith to do what we have to do? How can we live competently in the midst of suffering? Dr. Shaull gave the answer when he referred to the Magnificat. The kind of solidarity demanded of us is a solidarity that has fundamentally been inspired by the refugees themselves, the refugees in our midst, the people of Central America. They have become for us a source of resurrected hope, of revolutionary hope. In this vein, I want especially to stress the inspiration and hope that the women of Central America, the voiceless of the voiceless, offer us. I will also reflect very briefly on some of our own sisters here in North America.

What the refugees have brought to North America is a liberation gift. They have brought us this resurrected hope. The popular church of Central America has bequeathed to the world, and most eminently to its own people, an irreversible home in history. History, Gustavo Gutiérrez has told us, the poor know is theirs. Their hope is fundamentally a subversive act. The oligarchic rulers of Guatemala and of El Salvador cannot kill it off, cannot torture it to death, cannot bomb it into oblivion.

Fifty thousand murders have not eliminated insurgent hope in El Salvador. Hope lives in the highlands of Guatemala in spite of ethnocidal policies pursued ruthlessly from 1954 to this day. Not even the genocidal military offensives of 1983 quenched it. The endurance of revolutionary hope is what enrages dictators. They cannot understand its persistence.

Resurrected hope is indeed a hope that—like the phoenix—rises from the ashes, a fire death cannot extinguish. Fear of death is over-come by love of the people. Courage is less a personal attribute than a social gift of a people, the fruition of a decision, a commitment to be faithful to *El Pueblo* (the People) until the end.

María, a Salvadoran catechist, understood this when she said that we cannot avoid suffering and death but we can choose freely and consciously the side of our poor and oppressed people. In this way—as the Scripture says—no one takes my life from me; I give it freely. Such faithfulness forges a nobility and dignity of spirit that over-comes the banality of torture, death, and rape.

The recent history of Central America gives us innumerable sto-ries of women who are an unquenchable source of commitment and hope. There is, for example, the experience of Sister Victoria de la Roca of the District of Esquipulas in Guatemala. Dying of cancer when imprisoned and so weak that she could not dress, she was brought out in a robe to be executed, the soldiers already lined up for the ritual gang rape. Facing them calmly, she said: "I have been brought here, interrogated, and tortured because I sided with our people. I supported their opposition because I loved peace. If now you would violate me, come forward. I have been a consecrated reli-gious woman; and if for this you would violate me, come forward." Not one soldier moved. They slowly raised their rifles and in the teeth of death she snatched this dignity—simply, that she dictated the terms on which she died.

When I tell this story, I feel it necessary to clarify one point. I am not glorifying or exonerating victimhood. Actually, I do not think of her as a victim. She struggled to the very end to remain faithful, to tell the truth before power.

Too often this revolutionary legacy of the women of Central America becomes simply a martyrdom of victims. The women, left with the care and protection of the children and elderly in refugee camps and half-abandoned villages, continue to remain the voiceless of even the voiceless ones of Central America. But if the locus of God in history is discovered among the poor and the oppressed, then it is the women of Central America, triply oppressed, who most fully express and locate the suffering and resurrected hope of the God of history.

The indígena of Guatemala, the exiled Salvadoran women, the

women cotton pickers of Chinandega in Nicaragua bracing for bombing offensives, all these women, tenacious as the forgotten wildflowers clinging in the rocky crevices of the highlands, are the blooming presence of God in the blood-drenched earth of Central America.

These are the weak ones, the ones considered weak; and this is a story of their valor told me just a few months ago by a pastor recently returned from a refugee camp in El Salvador. The mothers, as many of you know, become very anxious when their sons reach adolescence because the Salvadoran military can then come to recruit them. On one such occasion, the officer in charge asked for a particular boy. All the mothers surrounded the shack, their arms locked, defying the order. The soldiers then began to beat them off with rifle butts. When all the women had fallen to the ground, their children joined arms and took their place around this young man. Even these soldiers left their prey that day. The weak ones, the silent ones, had won.

My final comment is again about the woman refugee, not just the woman in the camps but the woman refugee in exodus. She is the tree, rooted in a soil that is moist with the people's blood, who uproots herself, snapping off the tender wings of village life to journey into refugee camps—into exile, into liberated zones—to save a life, to struggle against death.

Even in exile she is the rooted tree from whom others will go forth and return. Until she is cut down, she is the one who will construct the social fabric of communal life, even in a wilderness. She is a strong tree. The sap of the people's lives runs in her veins. She is the backbone of the refugee camps in Honduras, El Salvador, and Mexico, as well as Guatemala.

The woman of Central America is a sign of hope, the incarnation of God's presence always. Even when the world falls apart, woman, like the cotton pickers of Chinandega, Nicaragua, lives as an embodiment of resurrected hope. When I visited Chinandega as a member of a group from the United States we went to some day camps way out in the middle of cotton fields that had been beautiful orange groves until Somoza's henchmen uprooted the trees to plant a crop from which he could squeeze more profit. Now there was not a single tree as far as the eye could see; all the way to the Honduran mountains, it was just wide open. We asked the mothers who used this little day care center, this miracle of the revolution for them, how they had managed before they had a place for the children to stay while they picked.

They began picking at 4:00 A.M., they explained. And they had done the best they could, they explained, almost embarrassed. They used to put the babies alongside them in the fields, covering them with a little cloth to keep lizards and rodents away. "That was before," they added proudly, "and now we have this."

Just then, an older woman, a cotton picker, pushed her way through the others who were describing how this revolutionary project had changed their lives. "Listen, my friends from the United States," she interrupted. "Why would your country wish to harm us? We are only a small nation, not even the size of one of your states, of your smaller states. Nevertheless, your leaders will send the Marines in as they did in Sandino's day."

She thought a moment and sighed before adding: "But this time, they will have to spill every drop of blood of Sandinismo in this country because now even the children will remember for us: *patria libre o morir* [a free nation or death]."

The old cotton picker then stepped back without much of a pause and said: "They say that Sandino said, 'If I die before the revolution triumphs, the little ants will crawl to me in the earth and they will tell me, "Sandino, the people have won!"' I think now the little ants are crawling to him in the earth and they are saying to him: 'Sandino, there's trouble, it's them again.' But that's not what I say to him. Instead, I say: 'Do not worry, Sandino. It's us again, *El Pueblo*.'"

PART THREE

Historical Perspectives on Sanctuary and Central America

CHAPTER 8

A HISTORICAL VIEW OF SANCTUARY

Francis X. Murphy

The ancient peoples behind our traditions—the Egyptians, the Hebrews, the Greeks, the Romans, and the barbarian nations—had concepts of sanctuary and asylum based originally, as you will see, on the need to prevent mob violence and family blood feuds. By fleeing to a shrine or temple sacred to a god, the accused or guilty party obtained immunity, within the precincts of the sanctuary, until the demands of justice could be met. This is really the background for our whole idea of sanctuary now. It has something to do with the sacred, with almighty God, and with God's presence in our community as well as in our world.

With the development of the Christian tradition, along with the claim to the inviolability of the sacred place—and thus the sanctuary afforded the accused or guilty individual—there gradually grew the right of intercession for the refugee on the part of the priest or custodian of the church or shrine.

An interesting incident in this regard is furnished by the great fourth-century patriarch of Constantinople, John Chrysostom. His mortal enemy, the eunuch Eutropius, as prime minister under the emperor Arcadius, abolished the right of sanctuary in spite of the patriarch. Less than a year later, Eutropius himself fell from grace and had to seek asylum in a church, where he would have been safe had he not imprudently left the sanctuary, even though it was he who had done away with the law of sanctuary. You can imagine the malicious joy with which Chrysostom, saint though he may have been, reflects upon this incident in the great oration he gave entitled, "A Homily on the Fall of Eutropius."

Interestingly enough, when in 392 the right of sanctuary was officially recognized in the code of Theodosius, great pains were taken to exempt from its protection public debtors, that is, the rich who were being pursued by the local *fisc*, the equivalent of our Internal Revenue Service. So way back in the fourth century there were problems with tax dodgers identical with those we're having now, and they were excluded from the right of sanctuary.

But long before the acknowledgment by Roman law of the Christian claim to sanctuary, Christians, following their Jewish heritage, had been practicing the concomitants of sanctuary. The concept of the love of neighbor comes directly out of the Jewish tradition in Leviticus and Deuteronomy. It is proclaimed by Jesus Christ as an essential practice of his religion and extended to all, including one's enemies.[1] In the earliest traditions, Christians were told to take care of prisoners and captives, who were given both public and private charity among Christ's earliest followers.

Evidence is supplied by primitive Christian documents that the visitation and care of prisoners and the persecuted were exercised by both deacons and the ordinary Christian. At the beginning of the second century, Ignatius of Antioch writes to his church of Smyrna: "When the Christians become aware that one of their numbers is a prisoner, or suffering for the name of Christ, they take upon themselves his needs, and if possible they free him"[2] Similar testimony is provided by Clement of Rome around A.D. 100 and witnessed by the pagan Lucian, who in his satiric *Peregrinus* says: "The Christians did not hesitate to bribe jailers in order to succor or even free the accused and prisoners."[3]

Tertullian, another theologian, at the end of the second century, says explicitly that the Christian has a duty to visit and care for and work for the liberation of prisoners,[4] a precept given support by the Apostolic Constitutions of Hippolytus and by Saint Cyprian of Carthage. Clement of Rome testifies further: "We know that many among us have given themselves up to chains in order to redeem others. Many have surrendered themselves to slavery and provided food for others with the money they received."[5]

With the Christianization of the empire after Constantine, the right of asylum in temples and sacred places was gradually taken over from the pagan shrines and transferred to churches and monasteries. A modified provision of this right was introduced into the codes of the Germans, the Visigoths, the Goths, the Alamanni, and other barbarian tribes. At first the inviolability of the sacred place was predominant. Gradually, however, the right of intercession by the bishop or priest became a principal function of the process of sanctuary and was pursued particularly in the canon laws of the church down through the centuries.

Eventually the papacy found it necessary to introduce a Congregation for Immunities, which dealt with the ecclesiastical privileges as well as the right of sanctuary and its abuses. Canon law upheld this right as a special function of religious charity despite the claims of the state to pursue justice, even though the churchmen could not base their claim to the right of asylum on either divine or natural law.

With the French Revolution and the secularization of modern states, the concept of sanctuary was gradually abandoned, although the Catholic church, for one, continued to claim the right of inviolability of its sacred premises. In the 1918 Code of Canon Law, however, a pragmatic view of modern political circumstances reduced the extension of this claim to one canon (1179) that maintained: "The church enjoys the right of asylum in the sense that guilty parties who there take refuge are not to be removed without the permission of the Ordinary of the place, or at least of the rector of the church, unless in the case of urgent necessity."

In effect, though not totally repudiating the ancient claim of the right to immunity, this canon so emasculates the claim as to come close to abrogating its possible use in our court system. The current Code of Canon Law, promulgated in 1984, again unfortunately, simply drops the claim.

There does not seem to be any tradition of the claim to sanctuary or asylum in the aid and abetment given to fugitive slaves in the preemancipation experience of our Underground Railway. Nevertheless, in our current concern for the rights and well-being of refugees, full attention—in my opinion—should be concentrated on the right of religious freedom maintained and guaranteed by the First Amendment of the Constitution, using as precedent the obligations professed and activated by the early Christians. This would require heroism, as we are all very well aware here and now.

But there is encouragement for such action in the statement of the Supreme Court in 1952 when Justice Douglas, legitimizing release/time for religious instruction, said:

We are a religious people whose institutions presuppose a Supreme Being. We guarantee the freedom to worship as one chooses. We make room for as wide a variety of beliefs and creeds as the spiritual needs of man deem necessary. We sponsor an attitude on the part of the government that shows no partiality to any one group, and lets each flourish according to the zeal of its adherents and the appeal of its dogma. When the state encourages religious instruction, or cooperates with religious authorities by adjusting the schedule of public events to sectarian needs, it follows the best of our traditions. For it then respects the religious nature of our people and accommodates the public service to their spiritual needs. To hold that it may not would be to find in the Constitution a requirement that the government show a callous indifference to religious groups. That would be preferring those who believe in no religion over those who do believe.[6]

The heroism required in our current pursuit of our religious beliefs and ideals takes its paradigm from the testimony of a great early church historian, Eusebius of Caesarea. He describes the intrepid early theologian Origen as being with the holy martyrs, not only while they were in prison, and not only while they were being examined up to their last sentence, but also after this when they were being led away to death, displaying great boldness and coming into close contact with danger.[7]

NOTES

1. John 13:34; Matthew 5:43–48.
2. Ignatius of Antioch, *Ad Smyr.* 6.
3. Lucian, *Peregrinus* 12.
4. Tertullian, *Ad Mart.* 1.
5. Clement of Rome, *1 EP to Cor.* 1.2.
6. *Zorach v. Clauson*, 343 US 306, 313–314, 1952.
7. Eusebius of Caesarea, *Hist. Eccl.* 6.3.4.

Response by Gus Schultz

It is important to remember that when we speak of sanctuary, we speak of it as *doing* sanctuary. We see it not as a place, not just as a single event, but as a process over a period of time. Part of the process of doing sanctuary is considering before making the decision.

Another part of it is proclaiming or declaring. It is very important to maintain a sense of this process. Sanctuary has been from the very beginning a grassroots process.

Some people consider sanctuary and never get to the point of proclaiming or declaring. And some people consider it and decide that it is not the proper thing for that congregation to do. It is important that we respect people's serious wrestling with this question and realize that those who go through that process of consideration have to make a decision about it. Most important, individual members are going to do things that they never did before. People who would not have heard the testimony of refugees will have had a chance to hear it, regardless of the decision they make later.

The Berkeley resolution of 1971, which incidentally was introduced by a Republican councilman, was the thing that led us in the Bay Area to begin looking at the sanctuary issue in relation to Central American refugees, and we did it at a Bible study group that met every Tuesday morning. We started talking about sanctuary and how it fit into what we were reading in the Scriptures. We discussed it, and we felt that this was something we ought to be considering with Central American refugees. Later, Marilyn Chilcote from Saint John's Presbyterian Church came to me and said that her group had been talking about this issue and that she had received a letter from John Fife in Tucson, Arizona, saying that his congregation was doing the same thing. We realized that people all over were doing sanctuary, and there was no official office, no national coordinator. Sanctuary is a grassroots thing, and it takes place on the local level.

Part of the reason I stress this is to tell you that the consultation among groups of sanctuary activists is not something that was created by a national group, by a national office, by a national coordinator, but something that has grown out of this process.

CHAPTER 9

A HISTORICAL VIEW OF
CENTRAL AMERICA
Murdo J. MacLeod

Central America has certain basic characteristics, dating in large part from the arrival of Europeans in the sixteenth century, that are important for understanding what is happening there today.

For the newcomers, the region was a disappointment. Compared to Mexico and Peru, it had few of the precious metals sought by the Spanish conquistadores. Consequently, those who settled there had to find a substitute *"el dorado"* that would to a lesser degree produce the wealth and social status necessary for returning with honor to the Old World.

Because of the lack of gold and silver, they emphasized—and the Spanish government encouraged them to emphasize—the production and export of primary raw materials. This economic emphasis very quickly divided the area, in particular the part that today constitutes the republics of Guatemala and El Salvador, into two zones. To the north and west is a mountainous area of poor material resources in which the majority of the people to this day are Indians, at least by cultural definition. They farm small plots and live a traditional, or what is held to be a traditional, way of life. To the south and east where the soils are better, agro-business or export industry moved in and very quickly acculturated most of the inhabitants or turned them into peasants.

In the Indian zone of the north and west, human beings are the main natural resource. For those who wish to extract wealth, the subsistence production system run by the Indian peoples is the main source of it. The production system is run by the traditional side of the economy, and the small minority that wishes to extract the surplus lives side by side with the laborers. The result is the evolution of what can only be described as a caste society. The minority, usually referred to as Ladinos in this area, extracts surplus out of an economy in which it does not participate. Accordingly, the two sides, or the two groups, who live in that area do not occupy the same agricultural areas, or even the same work places. Instead, there is a strict division between Indians and Ladinos, with the exploitation of the former by the latter.

In the other, more productive export zone to the south and east, the main economic characteristic is a boom and bust cycle. In this area, very rich volcanic soils have produced great wealth, a wealth that has been exported consistently. Over the years this zone has experienced five minibooms: cacao, indigo, cochineal, bananas, and coffee. Such monocultural export booms are extremely fragile for many reasons; one is the constant threat of competition. In coffee production, for example, competitors, or large-scale producers in other countries, may lower the world price. World price is the key factor, because it is essentially set outside these countries. Thus each boom is never dominated or controlled by native capital. Furthermore, the booms historically have seldom lasted longer than thirty years.

As a result of this fragility in the productive zone, the laboring classes are peasants. The working-class people in these areas, those who farm the coffee, those who farm the bananas, and so on, have had very little ability to organize in any consistent way to improve their standard of living. They are peasants who are alienated or pushed off the land because of the need for land concentration during the various booms. They are peasants because there is not enough surplus capital to support both the people who are leading these booms and the peasantry involved in them.

Because their wealth is derived from these monocultural primary export crops, Guatemala and El Salvador have failed to develop any genuine nationalistic middle class. In both countries, what some would think of as the middle class, or what Marxists would refer to as the bourgeoisie, is small. The major industries in these countries do not require large numbers of people who possess mechanical or other skills; this explains in part why in both countries, in this productive zone, development of the middle class has been inhibited.

The export economies of Guatemala and El Salvador share several other features in common. Because of the seasonal nature of so much of the export industry there is a heavy emphasis on seasonal migration of labor. Seasonal labor demands constitute one of the few forces that serve to link the two zones, the Indian zone and the monocultural export zone, together. The ties are forged by brokers, often Ladinos, in the Indian zone who act as *engancheros* (hirers of migrant labor) for the productive zones. As stated previously, the labor within the productive zone itself is a depressed peasantry held in various forms of serfdom or peonage, often landless, or almost landless, living from what might be described roughly as subsistence agriculture.

A second feature of the export-dominated area is the lack of a dynamic industry that would have created a central cohesive force there. This has led to fractionalism and the creation of a whole collection of minirepublics. As many of the leaders of Central America have recognized, this postindependence partitioning of the region has been a tragic liability and a tragic mistake. First of all, the republics are so small that they do not supply a large enough market within their boundaries to allow for the creation of service industries. In addition, in the case of Guatemala especially, about half the population is not a consuming population, that is to say, it does not buy large quantities of manufactured goods.

The inability to support the growth of local industries is not the only problem created by the existence of ministates. Perhaps even more troublesome is that small nations are prone to intervention. When there is a power vacuum, one of the great powers will certainly try to fill it. In Central America the great power in the nineteenth century was England; in the twentieth, it is the United States. These two powers have intervened militarily in Central America more than thirty times since independence in 1825. This persistent intervention has fostered increased instability and lack of cohesion. Many nonmilitary interventions have been just as damaging. A nineteenth-century British ambassador, Frederick Chatfield, used to state that his government's policy was to divide and rule, always to back the Federalists against the Centralists. He understood that it is much easier to deal with a bunch of sardines than with a fellow shark.

The absence of a middle class has also contributed to a lack of internal stability, because without a middle class there is no source for the evolution of complex pressure groups in the political arena. And this political void has been eagerly filled by military forces, who thus tend to dominate these less complex societies. The Central American militaries, then, have felt it their duty and their right to fill the legitimacy vacuum, and this has suited the elites. Lacking a middle class to bolster their position, the elites live with the threat of being surrounded by large numbers of deprived peasants. In consequence, they have traditionally allied themselves with the military to repress any aspirations for improvement or for social change coming from the peasantry. Because of this peculiar growth structure and the emphasis on monocultural export crops, these societies have failed to produce what we might call native capital. Not much money has accumulated, even among the local elites.

And so to fuel the next boom, the next cycle of agro-industry that comes along, Central American political and economic elites have had to look abroad. Even the most patriotic of Central American leaders have at times been forced, if interested in development at all, to seek development capital outside the region. And this is the typical trap, or *trampa*, as Guatemalans so often call it: foreign capital never comes in unattached; often, when threatened, it brings the Marines behind it. Moreover, when foreign capital dominates an economy, as it does in these countries—in Guatemala more than in El Salvador—it will not have as its primary responsibility the economic development of the local area.

It would be mistaken, nevertheless, to conclude that protection of U.S. direct economic interests is Washington's primary concern in Central America. U.S. investment in these small countries is much smaller than it is in Mexico, Argentina, or Brazil. It is most unlikely that any large or influential bank would fail if all the Central American governments were to default on their loans. The basic motivation of the U.S. government in this region seems to rest, rather, on prestige and control.

This brief overview of Central American history has perforce been schematic, selective of broad patterns that can be seen to have persisted for a very long time and that show little indication of changing. This persistence seems particularly observable in Guatemala, where the majority of the people have been struggling in one way or another against their government since 1956. The reason that the will of the majority cannot prevail is that the minority in power is always able to obtain outside support when the threat becomes too great, thus producing a vicious circle. The more pressure the people put on the government, the greater is the outside military support it gets, specifically from the United States, directly or through surrogates. The gruesome result is an indefinite continuation of the long and bloody war.

CHAPTER 10

THE REFUGEE CRISIS WITHIN CENTRAL AMERICA

Yvonne Dilling

The small Honduran village of Los Hernandez was quiet in the predawn hours of 18 March 1981. Only a few residents were awake and moving about their homes. It was an uncomfortable quiet, because during the previous three days, the rumble of distant war could be heard from beyond the mountain ridge in the direction of El Salvador.

Into that early morning quiet, a few dozen strangers arrived at one of the homes. They seemed hesitant to come right up to the house. They looked very tattered and dazed.

Beggars are a common sight in Honduras. But so many together was unusual. A Honduran man left his porch to see what the people wanted. As he rounded the bend at the stone fence marking the edge of his property, he stopped short. There were more than a hundred people slowly coming up the dusty path.

By nightfall that same day, more than three thousand refugees fleeing the war in El Salvador crowded into the yards, paths, and porches of Los Hernandez. The fifty homes in the village were filled with sick children and old folks. A few residents had closed their doors for fear of involvement in something they did not understand.

Honduran soldiers surrounded the village just as the sun set. They refused to let anyone leave the village. For subsequent months Los Hernandez was kept under close military surveillance.

Refugee experiences such as this are not a new phenomenon in Latin America's history. Since the beginnings of colonization by Spain, Britain, Portugal, and later the United States, countless events have provoked or forced societal upheavals. Although our history books have not explicitly described the affected people as refugees, particularly if they were Indians, they have been just that—refugees from natural disasters, conquerors, dictators, hunger, exploitation, and in general, from the sudden unraveling of their societal structures.

There is, though, a very new and significant element in the radical social changes that began sweeping through Central America in the 1970s and are continuing in the 1980s. Quite simply, it is the Bible, written in the language of the people and placed in the hands of the laity. This factor distinguishes this decade's Central American strife from that of the past several hundred years.

In previous times, whether refugees were fleeing the natural disasters of earthquakes or the human disasters of power-hungry generals, they turned to the church clergy for an explanation and for hope. Similarly, those who found themselves facing desperately needy people on their doorsteps looked to the church hierarchy for guidance on how to respond.

Today both these groups—those who find themselves homeless and on the run, and those who find needy people in their midst—are looking to their Bibles, their faith communities, and the guidance of the Holy Spirit within them to determine their response.

I believe it is most of all this grounding in the Bible that is bringing these Central Americans into the mainstream of history-making and -changing. The world is being altered by the experience of millions of lay people in Latin America trying to make sense of the oppressive circumstances in which they find themselves from the viewpoint of the Bible in their laps.

I speak from my particular experience of living a year and a half in the mountains of Honduras during 1981 and 1982, so I draw my examples and my reflections from two interrelated groups: Salvadoran Christians who were refugees and Honduran Christians who found desperately needy people in their midst. I will focus on the experience of Honduran Christians receiving the refugees; important insights from their experience can be applied to our work here in the United States.

I was a white, middle-class Protestant from the Anabaptist tradition, suddenly living in the midst of a poor, Catholic, Latino population. As I immersed myself in that experience and witnessed acts of Christian charity, I found myself drawing comparisons with my own family, my own church congregation, my own hometown, my own country.

One of my earliest experiences was a trip to a Honduran village, where I visited a very small home that sheltered five Salvadoran families. As I spoke with the six women and four men, including the Honduran host couple of the house—all of them with toddlers clamoring underfoot—my mind made rapid jumps between that home, that humble Honduran kitchen that fed some twenty-five people each meal, and the homes and kitchens of my family and friends. Women sharing the same kitchen amicably and men cultivating the land together and sharing farm tools, not for a day or a week, but for months on end.

I asked the women straight out if it was difficult for so many women to share one kitchen. The way they laughed, looking everywhere but at one another, assured me that although it was an emergency situation, it was the little things that tripped them up, too. They told me, however, that as they learned to focus on the bigger issues, they could put the small things aside.

One women stated the point succinctly. "It is hard to maintain our quarrels in the kitchen," she said, "when we are reciting the rosary together each night."

Through a multitude of experiences and interchanges such as that one, I learned that the immediate question was not, Would I or my family, my church, my town be able to respond to great need in such an open way? The more important question was, Would I be able, in my own North American context, to be so open to the Bible's guidance in my life as to allow for the total altering of my habits, lifestyle, and everything I am used to?

The Hondurans did not go looking for a new church project. The situation came to them and demanded a response. Some closed their eyes; some looked more closely.

The required response did not seem to offer any rewards, commendations, or praise. Rather, it very clearly looked as though to respond was to invite trouble in harsh form and degree. Little did they image the extent, however. Perhaps it was a blessing not knowing beforehand just how tight the screws of surveillance would turn. Had I known what was in store for me, I doubt that I would have chosen to be there.

I observed that when the Honduran people were confronted with this situation that could not be ignored, the Christians choose the extremes. Either they opened their hearts and homes, accepting all the unknown consequences, or they bolted the door and said, "Go elsewhere." Whatever their choice, all the people of faith experienced an acute tension between fear and spiritual trust.

To a large extent, the Christians who closed their doors were paralyzed by fear and then suffered from an additional internal conflict: the knowledge that they were acting in order to protect their own comfort, jobs, homes, family members, and indeed their very lives. Those of us who have never faced such an agonizing decision have no grounds on which to judge them, and those in that situation who have taken the other path of embracing the unknown will certainly feel compassion born of their own experience of suffering.

I worked with a team of local volunteers under the auspices of Caritas of Honduras. Most of my co-workers were born and raised in the immediate area. None of them had much more than a high-school education. Most were simple laborers. They ranged in age from those in the local youth group to a few whose hair had turned white and whose teeth were long gone. All were active in the Catholic church, and most were lay church leaders. They had a strong personal faith that they tried to live out daily; they had compassionate hearts.

Into their lives came the Salvadoran refugees. First there were a few dozen hiding in ravines in unpopulated areas. Those Hondurans who were distantly related to Salvadorans took the first small amounts of food out. The refugee numbers swelled, and then a few Caritas leaders took food out.

It took months, and the numbers swelled to more than a few thousand before someone took the bold step to say, "Come into my home." Remember the context in which they acted. There was a civil war going on in El Salvador. The Honduran government filled its radio reports with descriptions of subversion and communism tearing apart the fabric of Salvadoran society. As the Honduran families listened to the radio propaganda and looked into the faces of needy people, they faced a dilemma. They found the answer in the Scriptures, then sought the courage to follow the biblical mandate.

For those who embraced the task, for the Caritas volunteers and their families, the way was not easy. Indeed, it got harder than anyone imagined. But those who plunged most deeply into the work of simple biblical charity told me time and again that their faith had deepened beyond all boundaries, in ways they had previously not thought possible.

Three factors in the Honduran Christians' involvement are especially noteworthy for us. The first is that they grounded themselves solidly in the Scriptures. With each achievement they gave praise to God. They celebrated; they had fun. And whenever they encounted an obstacle or persecution, they turned to the pages of the Bible to once again get their bearings.

They scrutinized themselves and each other, identified errors and corrected them, and went on. They faltered. They rethought their involvement and went through the decision-making process again and again.

Some families burned out and pulled up stakes to move off to another part of the country. Some individuals found that family and friends turned from them. Most found themselves the targets of government suspicion and harassment. Many faced imprisonment and torture. Some were killed.

We never thought it would reach that point. We were very naive. The Honduran church also made mistakes, such as encouraging total investment by their lay catechists, then not moving in with full support when those lay leaders found their homes, livelihoods, and positions in the community threatened and destroyed.

At every new development, the Caritas team sought out one another to study the Bible and pray. When the obstacles and hardships evoked doubts in them, they would turn again to the Scriptures to make sure they had read them right. They could gain reassurance and hope from both the Scriptures and each other. It is crucial that we maintain this discipline.

Second, the Caritas team became aware that as months passed without any sign of change for the refugees, it was the poorer Honduran families that remained most faithful. Families with more material possessions were not more generous. Their possessions continually posed obstacles to their faith. Possessions competed with the refugees. Fear of losing everything they possessed made some Hondurans pull away from the work.

We in the United States must dare to confront our own attitudes toward our possessions and our propensity to define Christian charity as giving of our excess and no more. We must be willing to give more and to change our perceptions of what our basic necessities are. Our synogogues, congregations, and meetings must take seriously the responsibility to support those who give everything to help others.

The third point is one of attitude. It is very difficult to maintain a sense of the worth of the individual when the word *refugee* replaces the word *person*. Persons are more easily seen as brothers and sisters, as equals in the sight of God. Refugees tend to become inanimate objects toward which we direct our pious acts of charity, for which, we think, they should be exceedingly grateful.

The Honduran Caritas workers were able to see the worth of the individual, acknowledge it, and draw it out. Songwriter and singer Holly Near expresses it in one of her songs, "It could have been me, but instead it was you." Our tendency in this country is to say the opposite: "It could never happen to me." While even a trace of that condescending attitude lurks within us, we will not be able to fully embrace the Central American refugees among us as brothers and sisters.

A final observation: the Salvadoran refugees I worked with were eventually moved into a refugee camp far from the border. The Hondurans who had helped them were left with nothing but a bad reputation in the eyes of the local authorities. Harassment continued. Three of my co-workers were killed because of their refugee work, their children orphaned.

I correspond with some of the Caritas workers who survived. One might expect bitterness from them toward God, or at least toward the Catholic church hierarchy. But they are not bitter. They say that the biblical message continues to bear them up. They write that their suffering is not an unbearable burden. Their hearts have learned the deep and inexplicable joy of simply having done what was right. Hope for a better future is still very much theirs.

Honduran Christians experienced what they did because they turned to the Bible for direction when confronted by a difficult situation. When it became more difficult, they refilled their souls from the same Scriptures. It proved to be adequate nourishment.

What have we learned as we begin? For we really have just begun. I don't expect any of us to find a thousand people in our front yards overnight. Nor will the U.S. authorities respond so rapidly or with such intense brutality as the Honduran authorities did. Nevertheless, the way will not be easy for us. Already some of us are persecuted by U.S. authorities for opening our doors to refugees rather than turning away.

My hope is that we can ground ourselves in the Scriptures and be sustained and encouraged by the words we find there, and by one another. When we do, we also will experience the deep joy of having done what is right.

PART FOUR

Ethical, Legal, and Human Rights Perspectives on Sanctuary

CHAPTER 11

ETHICAL ISSUES OF THE INFLUX OF CENTRAL AMERICAN REFUGEES INTO THE UNITED STATES

James W. Nickel

A national movement to provide sanctuary for Central American refugees has emerged in the United States since 1982. Participants in this movement charge the Reagan administration with failure to comply with the right of sanctuary and are prepared to violate the law in order to provide transport and shelter to migrants from El Salvador and Guatemala. In this chapter, I will describe the sanctuary movement, present a philosophical perspective on the right to asylum, and discuss the justifiability of the sanctuary movement's use of civil disobedience and conscientious refusal.

The Sanctuary Movement

In recent years the U.S. government has generally denied refugee and "extended voluntary departure" status to applicants for political asylum from El Salvador and Guatemala. The Reagan administration's official explanation of this has been that these people are mostly seeking prosperity rather than refuge, and that it would therefore be foolish to grant them all asylum. These applicants, however, contend that their lives were endangered in their homelands by civil strife and government-sponsored death squads.

Religious leaders in Arizona and California reacted against these government policies in 1981 by helping Central American refugees enter and remain in the United States. In 1982, Rev. John Fife of the Southside Presbyterian Church in Tucson declared his church to be a sanctuary for Central American refugees, and churches in many parts of the country have since taken similar steps. As of early 1985, over two hundred churches are involved in this movement, providing refugees from Central America with transportation away from border areas, housing and food, and help in finding employment. Recently, several universities and university towns have declared themselves sanctuaries.

Efforts to aid refugees and opposition to U.S. military involvement in El Salvador and other Central American countries are often closely connected. Those receiving sanctuary often serve as speakers in programs to educate the American public about events in Central America.

Aiding, harboring, and transporting undocumented aliens is a federal offense, but many church people participating in the sanctuary movement believed that under the First Amendment's protection of religious freedom, they would be immune from criminal prosecution and that their church buildings could serve as "sanctuaries." Prior to the 1984 elections, the Reagan administration's actions seemed to confirm this view; no prosecutions were initiated. But in December 1984, sixteen leaders of the movement were indicted on federal charges of smuggling undocumented aliens and of conspiracy. These are felony charges under Section 274 of the Immigration and Nationality Act of 1952[1] carrying penalties of up to five years in prison for each count. Two people have been convicted and sentenced in Texas (Jack Elder and Stacey Merkt), and trials of others are proceeding.

Leaders of the sanctuary movement maintain that the government's policies toward Central American refugees are both morally and legally wrong. They say they are morally wrong because they violate the right to asylum as well as humanitarian principles that dictate giving aid to people fleeing persecution and civil strife. They further argue that the United States has a moral responsibility to assist people fleeing Central America because U.S. actions and policies have contributed to the strife that drives people from their homes.

The government's policies are said to be legally wrong because they are contrary to international and domestic law. In particular, they are held to be contrary to the United Nations Convention Relating to the Status of Refugees (1951). Like most subsequent documents, including the U.S. Refugee Act of 1980, this convention defines a refugee as one who has left his or her homeland and who has a well-founded fear of persecution, or that life or freedom would be threatened, on account of race, religion, nationality, membership in a particular social group, or political opinion. None of these documents, however, defines the meaning of "would be threatened" or "well-founded fear of persecution." The issue of *how probable* some harm to one's life or liberty must be is not addressed, and this leads to some of today's disputes about what these standards require.

The Reagan administration's official position on sanctuary can be summarized in four propositions. First, many migrants from Central America to the United States today are not primarily motivated by fear of persecution but by the desire to flee poverty and seek a better life. (One argument for this contention is that substantial Salvadoran migration to the United States preceded the civil war there by a decade or more.) Second, the United States recognizes a moral and legal obligation to accept refugees, but not to accept for permanent residence every arriving alien who claims to be a refugee. Third, procedures exist to determine qualifications for asylum on a case-by-case basis, and these procedures are fairly administered. Fourth, the 1980 Refugee Act and the UN protocol mandate asylum for specific targets of persecution, not for people simply endangered by a civil war.

These propositions put a good face on the administration's policies. The fact remains, nevertheless, that the INS systematically discourages Central Americans from requesting asylum. During 1984, for example, only 3 percent of requests from Salvadorans were approved, as contrasted with 14 percent of requests from Nicaraguans and 30 percent of requests from Poles.

Sanctuary workers were drawn into their present activities by meeting and talking to people who were afraid to go home to Central America and wanted help. They chose to believe these people rather than the U.S. government about the dangers they faced, and they opted for a broad rather than a narrow interpretation of "well-founded fear of persecution."

Speaking at the Eighth Annual National Legal Conference on Immigration and Naturalization Policy at the Center for Migration Policy, Staten Island, New York, in March 1985, Alan Nelson, director of INS, suggested that participants in the sanctuary movement were in no position to judge the validity of claims to asylum, to second-guess the INS and the courts. This is correct if it merely means that these people's judgments about the law are not authoritative intepretations with legal standing. But it is very incorrect if it means that citizens should always refrain from forming their own interpretations of key legal terms and acting in accordance with those interpretations. In contrast to Nelson's extremely legalistic view, I submit that all of us retain the right to second-guess our officials and their interpretations. Moreover, in the third section of this chapter I will defend the view that it is sometimes justifiable to violate official decisions, if we sincerely believe that they are wrong and if major violations of people's rights are at stake.

But that brings us to the question of whether the U.S. government violates human rights by operating with its current narrow conception of the right to asylum. I will try to answer this question in the next section by first presenting a general perspective on the role of human rights and then discussing the right to asylum.

The Right to Asylum

The right to asylum is the partner of the right to leave a country. The right to leave ensures that people who need to flee a country can get out; the right to asylum ensures that they will have a place to go. One of the main justifications for this pair of rights is easy to see; they jointly ensure that people will be able to protect themselves against foreseeable violations of their other rights by fleeing the country. When governments fail to protect the rights of their citizens, rights of self-help such as rights to flee and to defend oneself provide a second line of defense.

Defenders of the rights of migrants are sometimes hostile toward the contemporary international system because it gives states almost total discretion in deciding whom to admit. The right to asylum presents only a small exception to this rule, and hence migrant advocates may well prefer that the present categorical right to leave a country be matched with an equally categorical right to enter and reside in the country of one's choice.[2]

On reflection, however, one can see that it is not merely the narrow-minded insistence of states on their present prerogatives that precludes a general right to enter and reside in the country of one's choice. There are some good reasons for granting states substantial control over entry into their territories. The best of these reasons, in my opinion, pertain to the requirements of evolving and maintaining democratic institutions within a country. Earth as a whole is at present too large a unit for successful democratic institutions to operate; hence smaller political units are needed. Further, earth is extremely diverse in culture, language, and religion. If viable political communities are to emerge, at least some of these differences need to be accommodated in drawing political boundaries. For successful democratic institutions to evolve, a widely shared political culture needs to evolve as well. This is true of multi-ethnic as well as of more uniform countries. The evolution and maintenance of such a culture can be undermined if people who do not share this culture enter at a rate that makes enculturation impossible. Thus there are good grounds for allowing states to regulate the rate of migration into their countries. The discretion to do this, however, need not be unlimited.[3]

International human rights provide a counterbalance to the prerogatives of states. If the sovereignty of states responds to demands for community, order, and democracy, internationally recognized human rights respond to the most fundamental moral claims of individuals. Human rights—including the right to asylum—do not depend for their existence on their acceptance by governments; they exist independently as standards of argument and criticism. Some fundamental claims can be based simply on being a person with feelings, intelligence, choice, and a point of view of one's own. Since these claims are based on being a person rather than on being a member of some group, they can—when sufficiently serious—generate duties to assist that fall on countries other than the claimant's native land. These duties are not neutralized by national boundaries.[4]

Who can invoke the right to asylum? Although everyone has the right to asylum, it is appropriate to claim or invoke this right only when one believes that one needs to stay away from one's homeland or place of previous residence in order to avoid a violation, or a substantial probability of violation, of one's most basic rights. Exceptions to the scope of the right to asylum need to be made for common criminals who are fleeing punishment for their crimes. This matter commonly arises in the context of extradition policy.

The greatest problem in interpreting the right to asylum pertains to the degree of danger one must be subject to in one's homeland. The range includes

a. Being a personal target of violence (e.g., one's name is on a death list);

b. Being a member of a group that has been subject to much persecution (e.g., one is a trade unionist or university student in El Salvador);

c. Being subject to generalized violence (e.g., a civil war is being fought in one's immediate area of residence);

d. Having well-founded fears that political developments will occur that will put one in position a, b, or c.

This range is a continuum that goes from strong to weak claims to asylum.

The right to asylum is a narrow right; it gives people a very limited claim to enter countries other than their own. The justification for its narrowness is that it is necessary to accommodate the rights of states to regulate their territories and borders. Nevertheless, the right to asylum is an extension of very basic human rights, such as life, liberty, and freedom from torture. Flight is a way to protect these rights when governments become oppressive or break down, and the right to leave a country and to find asylum in nearby countries ensures that this way of escape will be open.

The already narrow right to asylum will not fulfill this role if it is interpreted very narrowly, if it only accepts people who have already been specifically targeted for persecution. Successful flight often requires foresight and advance planning, and thus those who wisely choose to flee in advance of persecution walk a tightrope: they must leave early enough to get out, but not so early that it is impossible for them to prove that they were likely targets of persecution. To provide a little footing on this tightrope, extremely narrow interpretations of the right to asylum have to be avoided. For example, if we require the ability to prove that one is a personal target of violence, we will make it impossible for the right to asylum to serve even minimally its functional role in the system of human rights—which is to ensure that people who need to leave a country will have someplace to go. If we require the threat to be personal, we will often require people to stay until it is too late.

Burdensome duties are often easier to bear if the beneficiaries are people with shared religious or political sympathies; hence countries tend to be more generous with asylum to those with whom they share an ideology. For example, Article 38 of the 1977 Constitution of the Soviet Union makes such restrictions explicit:

The USSR grants the right of asylum to foreigners persecuted for defending the interests of the working people and the cause of peace or for participation in the revolutionary and national liberation movement, or for progressive social and political, scientific, or other activity.

But if we think of people as having moral claims that are not forfeited by noncriminal political activity, and of human rights as requiring states to respond to these claims irrespective of nationality, then interpretations of the right to asylum that restrict it to one's religious or political allies are incorrect. This criticism applies not only to the Soviet Union, but also to the United States, in its tendency to give preference to asylum-seekers who are anticommunist.

Should one distinguish here between political and economic refugees? It is true that those whose claim is based on the danger of death, imprisonment, or torture have a stronger claim than those who merely wish to escape harsh conditions. Thus we can imagine that it will sometimes be legitimate for refugee policy to distinguish between applicants on these grounds, to limit the guarantee of safe haven to the former. But this is not the same distinction as the one between political and economic refugees. Under famine, the conditions threatening one's life may be economic; under authoritarian rule, the conditions that make one's life harsh (without threatening one's survival or liberty) may be political.

Who are the addressees of the right to asylum? The addressees of a right are the people or agencies who have duties or other liabilities under that right. The primary addressees of the right to asylum are governments, since they control the good in question, namely, access to safe territories. If one has fled one's homeland into country C, it is the government of C that will be obligated by one's request for asylum.

If someone is being attacked and screams for help, people in the vicinity may have obligations to aid the victim as well as liberties and immunities that protect them in doing so. Similar duties may exist in assisting those who are fleeing threats to their lives and liberty. Those who are in a position to provide such assistance to persons seeking asylum might be thought of as secondary addressees.

When a request of asylum is made, what must be done? Suppose that a person A, who has a prima facie claim to asylum, has requested asylum from country C. What duties does C have to A? First, C has a duty to not return A to the country A fled, unless and until A's claim proves ill-founded. This is a negative duty, a duty to refrain from acting in a certain way. Second, C has a duty to give full and fair consideration to A's claim. This is a positive duty, a duty to provide a certain form of benefit. What it involves will be discussed later.

When an asylum-seeker's claim has met a reasonable standard of proof, what duties does the country have? Here we can imagine that country C has evaluated A's claim and found that A is indeed threatened in his or her country of origin. What then are C's duties? I submit that they are the following: first, not to return A to the country he or she fled; second, to offer A a place of permanent or extended residence unless one is clearly available elsewhere. Note that the negative duty not to return A to his or her homeland implies, in this situation, a positive duty to offer a place of residence. Countries often try to "pass the buck" in regard to offering a place of residence; they try to push the burden of doing this onto another country. It is hard to say that this is never permissible, but it does need to be restrained. Relevant considerations here seem to be: the space that C has available for new residents; the rate of recent immigration to C; and whether C has borne a fair (or larger than fair) share of the burden of resettling refugees in recent years.

What is the weight of the right to asylum? The weight of a right is its ability to prevail over competing considerations. One argument for assigning very substantial weight to the right of asylum runs as follows: Effective flight from persecution is frequently essential to protecting fundamental rights such as rights to life and liberty. The effective ability to flee requires that one have some place to flee to. If one is unable to leave a country where one's basic rights are endangered, or is immediately returned to it upon escape, one's flight will be unsuccessful. Thus, the most basic rights depend for their protection on the right to asylum. If the effective implementation of one right is a necessary means to the implementation of another, then the weight of the second is at least as great as the weight of the first. Thus, whatever weight is possessed by the most basic rights is also possessed by the right to asylum. Since the right to asylum has the same weight as the weightiest right, it is a very weighty right.[5]

If the right to asylum has the great weight that this argument contends, then it cannot be outweighed by ordinary considerations of administrative convenience or cost. If we take the idea of a weighty right seriously, then we cannot simply ignore such rights because they would increase the burdens of the courts or because they would increase the flow of migrants to the United States. But this seems to be exactly what the Reagan administration is doing.

The right to asylum, since it is weaker than a general right of migrants to enter and reside in a country of choice, presupposes some selection process whereby applications for asylum will be evaluated. Because of the weight of this right, careful and fair procedures are demanded by elementary principles of procedural justice.

The Reagan administration's almost wholesale denial of refugee status to those fleeing conflicts in Central America seems difficult to defend on procedural grounds. Persons charged in the United States with crimes serious enough to have penalties that threaten life or liberty are protected by the right to due process, which requires elaborate measures to produce a fair and accurate result. They are also protected by the presumption of innocence, which requires that the government bear the burden of proof. Even illegal aliens charged with felonies have this right and are entitled to the same procedures. Seekers of asylum facing similar dangers seem entitled to similar procedural protections—given the seriousness of sending people home to face risks of persecution and death. Just as we insist that our government bear the burden of proof in proving criminal guilt, we ought to insist that our government bear the burden of proof in proving its often glib contention that most Central American refugees are fleeing from poverty rather than persecution. Just as we say that it is better that many guilty go free than that one innocent person be convicted, we can say that it is better that many immigrants fleeing poverty be admitted than that one refugee fleeing persecution be sent back.

A possible response to this is that administrative procedures of this sort will be too expensive, that we cannot afford to provide aliens with the same protections we provide to those charged with serious crimes. Two things should be said in response to this. One is that, although we might prefer to spend these resources elsewhere, we can in fact afford to spend more money on fairer procedures within the immigration system. The scale of expenditure in question would be in the tens of millions, not in the billions. The second response is that if the administration wishes to avoid many of these costs, another option is available. This option is conferring extended voluntary departure status on aliens from El Salvador.

Civil Disobedience and Sanctuary

My concern in this section will be with questions about civil disobedience and whether one can justify breaking the law in order to provide sanctuary for undocumented refugees. Those who break the law in order to provide sanctuary are likely to be charged with acting unethically by deliberately breaking the law and thereby undermining respect for the law.

Before trying to deal with this criticism, we should attend to the strenuous contention of some people in the sanctuary movement that they are upholding rather than violating U.S. law, and hence are not engaging in civil disobedience. Many people involved in providing sanctuary to Central American refugees believe that the current policies concerning Central American refugees are unlawful because they are contrary to international treaties that the United States has ratified and that are the supreme law of the land.

This problem is not new or unique to the sanctuary movement. Since it is often hard to know exactly what a complex legal system requires in a particular case, and to know whether the laws and policies governing that case are constitutionally valid, it often happens that those who engage in principled violations of the law aren't sure whether they are really violating the law, or really violating a *valid* law.

For example, civil rights workers during the sixties frequently believed that the statutes they were violating were constitutionally invalid—and the Supreme Court eventually endorsed that view in many cases. In retrospect we may say that many of the people who participated in sit-ins and demonstrations didn't break any laws. But *pro*spectively, when one needs to evaluate one's proposed actions, it is better to conceive civil disobedience broadly enough to include both cases in which one is certain that one is violating the law and cases in which the legal situation is murky and one believes that there is a significant possibility that one is violating the law. In this way, the moral problem arising should it turn out that one's legal judgments were wrong will have been taken into account from the beginning.

Civil disobedience is a communicative act, a form of public expression, in which one deliberately and publicly violates a law in order to communicate to citizens and officials one's profound disagreement with a law or policy. Mounting a legal challenge to the law may also be part of one's objective. Since someone engaging in civil disobedience desires to communicate to a large audience and to demonstrate sincerity and conscientiousness, arrest and prosecution are often desired as components of effective civil disobedience. For similar reasons, civil disobedience is likely to involve nonviolent violations of the law.

Conscientious evasion, unlike civil disobedience, is not intended as a communicative act; it is primarily intended as a way of avoiding the evil consequences of a bad law, or of the bad administration of a law. Conscientious evaders do not seek publicity for their actions, and being prosecuted is something they typically seek to avoid.[6]

I suspect that some sanctuary providers have thought of what they were doing as conscientious evasion, in which the main goal is to help refugees, and others have thought of what they were doing as civil disobedience, in which the main goal is to change law or policy. The recent prosecutions may force sanctuary workers to make up their minds about exactly what their primary goals are. Those whose focus is mainly on helping refugees may prefer conscientious refusal and the operation of an "underground railroad." On the other hand, those who are oriented toward changing U.S. immigration policies and ending U.S. involvement in Central America may prefer programs in civil disobedience.

Next I will review a few of the main positions on the moral justifiability of "principled disobedience," which I take to include civil disobedience and conscientious refusal. Advocates of a conservative position hold that in a constitutional democracy, where political channels exist for changing bad laws, principled disobedience is never morally justifiable—even if one's cause is morally correct. In the constitutional democracy, they argue, citizens have a strong moral obligation to obey the law. This obligation is the other side of the legitimate authority of democratic governments. Those who violate the law on principle (e.g., in order to provide sanctuary to undocumented refugees) are acting undemocratically by deciding individually what ought to be decided collectively through democratic institutions. Principled disobedience often has bad consequences, since it tends to undermine respect for law and thus undermine social and political order and ultimately the rule of law.

As Martin Luther King, Jr., often reminded people, great injustices are often carried out through law—even in constitutional democracies. The conservative view is vulnerable to the argument that its absolute duty to obey the law is implausible in a world where injustices are regularly carried out through legal means. To avoid this criticism, a more moderate position might allow that principled disobedience is permissible in extreme cases even in constitutional democracies, but it might require that all legal means of changing the law have been exhausted before one engages in principled disobedience.

The liberal position recognizes the moral claims of respect for law, democratic institutions, and an orderly society but holds that these moral claims need to be balanced against the human rights of individuals. In particular, the liberal position holds that principled violations intended to evade or protest laws that violate human rights are often justified, even when not all possible democratic means of changing the law have been exhausted. Through principled disobedience the rights of particular individuals can be protected, effective protests can be mounted, and governments can be made aware that people will not tolerate grave injustices and violations of rights.

Advocates of the liberal position criticize the conservative positions in several ways. If there is a general moral obligation to obey the law, they say, it is not absolute or unlimited—even in a democracy. Our commitment to obey the will of the majority, or that of their elected representatives, is within a framework of constitutional and human rights. And these rights set limits to what the majority, or the government, can do. Further, many theorists have suggested that principled disobedience is complementary to democracy; it is a means by which people can let the strength of their opposition be known.

In the case of the sanctuary, the democracy argument has severely limited impact. It is not as though there has been a referendum on just this issue, so that we know that the majority of American people don't want to admit Central American refugees. Nor do we know that most federal officials endorse present policies. All we know is that these policies are endorsed by the INS and by some people in the Reagan administration—and that they haven't been overruled by Congress.

The alleged bad consequences of principled disobedience for order and the rule of law should not be ignored, since the existence of order and respect for the law is one of the things that makes the United States attractive as a place of sanctuary. But the scale of such bad consequences seems greatly exaggerated by conservatives—particularly if we are talking about nonviolent violations. Our experience with principled disobedience to protest injustice has not shown it to lead to widespread lawlessness. Our system of law and obedience to law is not so fragile, and the consequences of law violations by people helping to provide sanctuary so large, that we need fear significant damage to our legal order.

The moderate conservative claims that, in order to respect law, we have to respect laws that we disagree with by trying to change them through ordinary political means before we engage in extraordinary means like civil disobedience. A more plausible criterion is that one not engage in principled disobedience unless one has well-founded beliefs that efforts to change the policy through ordinary political means will fail in the foreseeable future. The concern with timeliness is not merely a matter of impatience but is, rather, rooted in the worry that delay will lead to further suffering and injustice.

NOTES

1. 8 U.S.C. 1324.
2. See Roger Nett, "The Civil Right We Are Not Ready For: The Right of Free Movement of People on the Face of the Earth," *Ethics*, vol. 81, no. 3 (April 1971), pp. 212–227.
3. On issues about membership, see Michael Walzer, *Spheres of Justice* (New York: Basic Books, 1983), pp. 31–63.
4. See my paper "Human Rights and the Rights of Aliens," in Brown and Shue, eds., *The Border That Joins* (Totowa, N.J.: Rowman & Littlefield, 1983), pp. 31–48. See also "Are Human Rights Utopian?" *Philosophy and Public Affairs* 11 (1982), pp. 246–264.
5. This pattern of argument is adapted from Henry Shue, *Basic Rights* (Princeton: Princeton University Press, 1980).
6. The distinction between civil disobedience and conscientious refusal is drawn by John Rawls, *A Theory of Justice* (Cambridge, Mass.: Harvard University Press, 1971).

CHAPTER 12

REFUGEES AND HUMAN RIGHTS
William L. Wipfler

The quality of an international system is well judged by the condition of its refugees. If that is true, then the contemporary international system can be characterized as impoverished and on the way to bankruptcy.

The refugee problem throughout the world represents a crisis of startling proportions. It is estimated that registered refugees throughout the world number 12.6 million, and identified displaced persons, that is, individuals uprooted within their own borders, represent 5 million. The flight of this staggering number of human beings is a clear and visible witness to the tragic violations of human rights in their countries of origin.

The tragedies are compounded by the dangers they often face in the place of refuge. The government in the country of refuge may be an ally of the government from which they fled; or they may not be accepted as refugees and be threatened with deportation. They may be rejected for racial, ethnic, political, ideological, or religious reasons. Under these and myriad other circumstances that are encountered by refugees, there is a constant threat of continued violation of their most fundamental human rights.

Patricia Weiss Fagen of the Refugee Policy Group in Washington has written that individual human rights are protected ordinarily through the mediation of governments. However, refugees and stateless persons, that is, persons who can no longer claim protection of basic rights from their national government, because they have fled, and who have not been accepted as eligible for protection by any other state, are extremely vulnerable to continued human rights abuses. This is why the definition and determination of who is a refugee is of such importance in discussing the international law dealing with refugees and human rights. The search for a definition is comparatively recent. It came about solely as a result of an attempt to discover ways to deal with the problem of displaced persons after the Second World War.

The United Nations established the International Refugee Organization (IRO) in 1946. It had a four-year mandate, and it was believed that it could deal with the refugee problem that confronted it within that period. In the constitution of the IRO, refugees were cited not by definition but by nationality. In other words, specific groups of people were recognized and spoken about. A major element in the constitution, however, was the embodiment of a principle, probably the basic principle of all refugee protection throughout the world, called nonrefoulement, that is, no refugee with valid objections should ever be compelled to return to his or her country of origin. The first valid objection listed in the IRO constitution was persecution or fear based on reasonable grounds of persecution because of race, religion, nationality, or political opinion. This would later become a core element in the definition of a refugee.

When the IRO mandate ran out, it was obvious that many postwar problems, along with new problems that were arising, still needed attention. Accordingly, in January 1950, the UN initiated a process that in the following year brought the completion and approval of the most rapidly drafted convention ever produced by that body: the Convention on the Status of Refugees. This international agreement made several important advances in the protection of refugees. First, it is of utmost importance to recognize the context into which the drafters placed the new convention, that of recently accepted human rights standards. The preamble reads as follows:

Considering that the charter of the United Nations and the Universal Declaration of Human Rights approved on 10 December 1948 by the General Assembly have affirmed the principle that human beings shall enjoy fundamental rights and freedoms without discrimination. Considering that the United Nations has on various occasions, manifested its profound concern for refugees and endeavored to assure refugees the widest possible exercise of these fundamental rights and freedoms. . . .

What was clearly implied by the inclusion of these references was that refugees could make a claim for the protection of their human rights based on their humanity, not on their nationality. Furthermore, the convention included a significant improvement in the definition of a refugee. Article One said that the term *refugee* means any person who is outside any country of such person's nationality or, in the case of a person having no nationality, is outside any country in which such person last habitually resided, and who is unable or unwilling to return to, and is unable or unwilling to avail himself or herself of the protection of that country because of persecution or a well-founded fear of persecution on account of race, religion, nationality, membership in a particular social group, or political opinion. In addition, the convention strengthened the protection of refugees against refoulement, against expulsion from the country of refuge, against the return of refugees to "the frontiers of territories where life or freedom would be threatened on account of race, religion, nationality, membership of a particular social group, or political opinion."

Unfortunately, that convention limited all its protection to those who were refugees prior to the events of 1 January 1951. However, in 1967, that clause was nullified, thereby making the convention applicable to all refugees embraced within that very important definition. Although the convention and protocol were significant steps in protecting refugees, it must be kept in mind that they were brought into being out of the experience of Europe after the Second World War. And, though the emphasis in refugee questions has always been on humanitarian motivation, it is clear that ideological issues, the East-West conflict, and economic conditions have played a major role in governmental decisions on the treatment and reception of refugees.

Until the United States incorporated the UN definition into domestic law in the Refugee Act of 1980, the practice of the Immigration and Naturalization Service was to grant refugee status automatically to persons who fled communist countries, on the assumption that living in a communist country was persecution enough. Those who escaped from repressive governments friendly to the United States, however, were given no such presumption. Instead, they were almost always viewed as economic refugees, namely, individuals unwilling or unable to accept the hardships of the development process in their homeland. In addition, the fact that the United States and Western European governments provide the bulk of the support for international refugee machinery means that their influence often conditions the effective application of international agreements. In an interesting monograph, Charles Keely notes, for example: "France, a UN charter member, gave clear signals that refugees from the Algerian war were not designated refugees because such a designation would have been equivalent to labeling France a persecutor."[1]

A similar situation has arisen in the treatment of Central American refugees by the United States. To accept Guatemalans and Salvadorans as refugees would be an admission that the United States is aiding governments engaged in the widespread violation of the rights of their citizens. Not only has the United States denied asylum or extended voluntary departure status to these refugees inside this country, it has also pressured the United Nations High Commissioner for Refugees (UNHCR) to undertake a program of repatriation (the expenses of which are to be paid for by USAID) of Salvadoran refugees located in camps in Honduras.

The office of the United Nations High Commissioner for Refugees, which is responsible for the implementation of the convention and protocol and for the protection of refugees, has warned of a number of trends that threaten to undermine the international agreements and further limit or violate the fundamental rights of refugees. There is the additional problem that almost all international law—except for the relatively few matters that can be adjudicated before the World Court—depends on world public opinion for its enforcement. The conventions and protocols of the UN do not provide for penalties; there is simply the commitment of the signatories to observe them. Everything depends on the spirit with which the signatories commit themselves and the extent to which they are affected by world public opinion. All the UN and its agencies can do is to help create a sense of pressure in world public opinion against nations who contravene provisions of conventions they have signed.

In its most recent meeting, November 1984, the executive committee of the UNHCR denounced serious violations and disregard of the physical safety of refugees and seekers of asylum in many parts of the world. The committee particularly expressed concern for the repeated abrogation of the principle on nonrefoulement, and increasingly restrictive policies for granting of asylum. They also denounced the increase military and armed attacks against refugees and refugee camps, as well as piracy upon and failure to rescue refugees at sea. Furthermore, Paul Hartling, the High Commissioner, introduced a serious caution when he spoke to a distinguished group of journalists in February 1984: "Xenophobia is more than just a fashionable word. It is a chronic illness which, if left unchecked, may have far reaching consequences for the family of nations. Xenophobia is the selfish egocentric ill will against people who are different and therefore against foreigners."[2]

Insofar as the refugee is concerned, present restrictive trends in many countries show us what disastrous consequences xenophobia may have. Thus we see governments being increasingly reluctant to admit refugees. Numerous governments that have hitherto followed generous policies have in recent times demonstrated a most distressing tendency to apply stringent deterrent measures with the evident aim of stemming the flow of asylum seekers. Such measures run counter to the humanitarian objectives of international action in favor of refugees. The U.S. government has not been above using and nurturing the xenophobia and racism that exist in U.S. society.

On 20 June 1983 the President, in seeking support for his military policy in Central America, told an audience in Mississippi that if U.S. strategy didn't succeed, "the result could be a tidal wave of refugees, and this time they'll be feet people, not boat people, swarming into our country, seeking a safe haven from communist repression to our south."[3] At approximately the same time, the U.S. Coordinator for Refugee Affairs, Ambassador H. Eugene Douglas, issued a congressional briefing paper on refugees and potential refugees in and from Central America. He offered estimates of the number of refugees that would come north as the republics of Central America from Panama to Mexico fell to Marxism. The House Republican Research Committee distributed a document entitled "Central American Refugees: Social and Economic Consequences for the United States." It calculated the influx of refugees to reach 7.21 million minimum, at a cost of $25,235,000 to the taxpayer and an increase in unemployment in the United States to 12.9 percent.

By contrast, some have suggested that the definition of refugee should be expanded to include economic refugees. The problem is not simply the difficulty of defining what constitutes an economic refugee. There is no willingness on the part of the international community at this time to agree on a common policy toward economic refugees. Furthermore, the present definition of refugee does not even raise the issue of who may have exported the violence that created the conditions from which the refugee flees. It identifies the refugee as fleeing from fear of persecution but ignores the possibility that the persecutors may have been armed by the very country to which the refugee is fleeing. The exporting of political terror occurs in the same way as the exporting of economic exploitation. How a particular country will react will vary according to political circumstances. The United States, for example, does not complain about fund-raising for Ethiopian economic refugees in the Sudan. One wonders what its attitude would be if it found itself besieged by millions of refugees escaping from a famine just as serious. Would it close its borders? It has not suggested that the Sudan should close its borders.

Each situation is dealt with differently, and each nation has certain parameters within which it functions. It is significant, for example, that impoverished countries are often more willing to accept refugees without attempting to distinguish the political from the economic. Mexico has great difficulty at the present time in dealing with the refugees within its borders. It has been harsh on the Guatemalans, but that is the result of pressure from both the Guatemalan and the U.S. governments. There are also internal pressures, because Guatemala borders on Mexico. It has been less strict on Salvadorans who are passing through, although they also have problems. Historically, it has been generous in accepting Spanish Republicans, Chileans, Uruguayans, and people from other countries.

The way in which each country views the foreigner is important. I believe, for example, that the reference made by the UNHCR to xenophobia was intended for the United States, even though he did not mention it by name. It is noteworthy that he made it in February 1984, at a time when the United States was creating greater restrictions for granting asylum and was deporting large numbers of Central Americans. The point he was making was that the United States was making an excessive distinction between economic and political refugees, thereby violating the spirit of the law. Human rights issues cannot be decided on strictly legal bases. It is a matter of spirit, not of technical definition.

A *New York Times* editorial commenting on President Reagan's warning of "a tidal wave of refugees" described these tactics as scaremongering. The present Reagan policy, it said, risks creating more not fewer refugees. It is also worth noting that the President's speech and both of the documents referred to earlier raise fears regarding a potential invasion of the United States by Central American refugees; however, all three ignore the actual presence of as many as five hundred thousand Salvadorans and Guatemalans who are already here seeking safe haven from the repression of governments friendly to the United States.

The behavior of the present administration toward refugees from many corners of the world and especially Central America—detaining them and subjecting them to judicial abuse, denying them refugee status, and finally deporting them to their own countries and possible persecution and death—has been a flagrant contravention of the human rights of refugees assured by international law. The United Nations High Commissioner for Refugees' *Manual for Application of the Convention and Protocol* makes it clear, for example, that refugees who cannot escape with documentation in hand, with proof that they are persecuted, should be given the benefit of the doubt in their interviews. Instead, countless arguments have been advanced by U.S. government spokespersons to justify the denial of a humanitarian response and the acceptance of such individuals as refugees. Conditions in El Salvador and Guatemala are not sufficiently hazardous, they claim, to warrant the granting of asylum or extended voluntary departure status to Salvadorans or Guatemalans. They insist that Salvadorans and Guatemalans are largely here for economic reasons, that granting special status will encourage heavier waves of illegal immigration, and that Central Americans coming to the United States should seek asylum in other countries through which they pass.

Senator Alan Simpson, chairperson of the Senate Immigration Committee, has stated in a letter to a constituent that if the Salvadorans were political refugees, they would stay in refugee camps in Honduras, where they would be safe. The logic of his statement reveals that he recognizes that they are indeed political refugees, since otherwise they could not claim admission to a refugee camp. However, what he overlooks is that when refugees begin the journey for refuge, the issue of first asylum is not on their minds. First asylum is the place where refugees stop and ask to be accepted as refugees. Under the UN manual, which guides those who have to interview refugees in order to make a decision about granting asylum, the person requesting must be given the benefit of the doubt. A person fleeing from terror, fleeing because of fear, may not have made a decision about where to finally stop.

In addition, we know that Honduras is not the most hospitable of places for many of the refugees. In some of the camps there is the danger of incursions from Salvadoran troops across the border, persecution by the Honduran government, and a very clear activity on the part of the Honduran government to limit the number of refugees. The mediating body that makes the decision in each case is the United Nations High Commissioner for Refugees. Almost always its ruling is definitive in stating who is a refugee. In both Honduras and Mexico, it is the United Nations High Commissioner who has established camps and provided protection. On two occasions the UNHCR has actually called the United States into question for refoulement, that is, the deportation of Salvadoran refugees back to their place of persecution.

Senator Simpson's argument is consequently not a very solid one. Refugees are never considered to be in a position to make a decision about first asylum. In other words, when fleeing, they flee to a point where they can at least stop and seek safe haven. Whether they stop in Honduras or go from the frying pan into the fire by stopping in Guatemala—and there happen to be seventy thousand in Guatemala—or if they go on to Mexico or to the United States, is not, under the terms of the definition of a refugee, of great importance in the final determination.

Spokespersons for the U.S. administration tell us that foreign policy considerations weigh against granting asylum or extended voluntary departure. They claim that those who are allowed to remain under a special status may seek to settle permanently. And, most cynically of all, they state that persons who are deported are in no more danger than those who never left their homeland. These arguments are presented in spite of the fact that every major human rights organization, Amnesty International, Americas Watch, and the International Commission of Jurists, has denounced the acute level of official violence, the frequency of torture and indiscriminate killing, and the generalized repression of Guatemala and El Salvador.

The office of the United Nations High Commissioner for Refugees has declared that all Salvadorans who have left their country since early 1980 are in a refugee-like situation and should be provided protection from refoulement. The lawlessness of the U.S. administration is highlighted not only by the criminal act of mining Nicaraguan ports, the hiring and paying of a counterrevolutionary mercenary army, the equipping and training of an army in El Salvador that has taken the lives of forty-six thousand unarmed civilians—all of which are violations of international law—but also by its denial of rights to bona fide refugees within our borders. The words of the great jurist, the Supreme Court justice Louis Brandeis, should come to that administration as a solemn warning: "Our government is the potent, the omnipresent teacher. For good or ill, it teaches the whole people by its example. If the government becomes a lawbreaker, it breeds contempt for the law. It invites every person to become a law unto himself. It invites anarchy."[4]

NOTES

1. Charles B. Keely, *Global Refugees' Strategy: The Case for a Development-Oriented Strategy* (New York: The Population Council, 1981), p. 2.
2. Paul Hartling, "Refugees: Victims of Xenophobia." Opening Statement to a Round Table Organized by the United Nations High Commissioner for Refugees, Palais des Nations, Geneva, 24 February 1984, p. 1.
3. Francis X. Clines, "Reagan says his opponents risk Central America influx," *New York Times*, 21 June 1983, p. A14.
4. *Changing Course: Blueprint for Peace in Central America and the Caribbean* (Washington, D.C.: Policy Alternatives for Caribbean and Central America [PACCA], Institute for Policy Studies, 1985), p. 63.

CHAPTER 13

THE CONSTITUTIONAL AND LEGAL ASPECTS OF THE REFUGEE CRISIS

Gary MacEoin

A major reason for the existence of the sanctuary movement is the systematic violation of the constitutional and legal rights of Central American refugees by the Immigration and Naturalization Service (INS) at all levels, including in deportation hearings in its administrative courts.

Up to about twenty-five years ago admission of refugees was governed by custom and administrative procedures that produced reasonably equitable results. Changed conditions in the countries to our south have radically altered the situation, and today the United States finds itself in violation of domestic and international law, exposing thousands of innocent persons to the risk of persecution, torture, and death.

The 1980 Refugee Act, incorporating the provisions of the UN Convention and Protocol on Refugees, was based on an assumption that had already lost much of its validity, namely, that the United States would continue to be—as it had been—a country of second settlement for refugees who, having fled their homes to one country, would there be processed for orderly admission to the United States. Before the end of 1980, 125,000 uninvited Cubans—the Marielitos—had landed. Fifty thousand Haitians had been captured, and unknown additional thousands had entered without inspection. And from Central America had come the first thousands of an avalanche that has now probably passed the half million mark.

The 1980 act had eliminated the preferential treatment provided in the 1962 law for persons fleeing a communist regime. The cold war mentality behind that provision had, however, not changed. "Despite posturing to the contrary," says Michael Maggio of the

Council on Hemispheric Affairs, Washington, D.C., "geopolitical considerations rather than genuine humanitarian concerns continue to shape U.S. policy toward those who flee repression, as well as toward repressive regimes."[1] The criterion is citizenship. An Afghan or a Pole gets preferential treatment. Haitians, Guatemalans, and Salvadorans are categorized as economic refugees and, as such, outside the protection of the UN Convention and Protocol on Refugees, no matter how strong the evidence that they are political refugees. A study conducted by the INS in June and December 1982 found that "although the Refugee Act of 1980 abolished the country of national origin test for refugee/asylum status, for foreign policy or other reasons the criterion may still be overriding." It is "unclear," it noted, "what the statutory basis for such a determination is." It may be unclear to the INS but not to many immigration lawyers. There is *no* statutory basis for that practice. It is unlawful. The same study goes on to note that "certain nationalities appear to benefit from presumptive status while others do not." Specifically, for a Salvadoran to receive a favorable asylum advisory opinion from the State Department, she or he must have "a classic textbook case." Yet the State Department sometimes recommends favorable action when the applicant cannot meet the individual "well-founded fear of persecution" test, such as when seven Polish crewmen jumped ship in Alaska in December 1981. "Even before seeing the asylum applications, a State Department official said: 'We're going to approve them.' "[2]

The same double standard applies to extended voluntary departure (EVD). This administrative procedure, without adjudicating the issue of whether or not an individual is entitled to political asylum, authorizes residence and the right to work for as long as conditions in the person's homeland would threaten death or persecution if he or she returned. EVD has been granted extensively in recent years to Ethiopians, Hungarians, Afghans, Poles, and others. Not only does the administration deny it to Central Americans and Haitians, but it opposes the DeConcini-Moakley bill now in Congress that would mandate EVD for a limited time for Salvadorans now in the United States.

Where the geopolitical considerations of the administration are most obvious is in the highly publicized granting of asylum to stars of tennis and other sports who defect from the Soviet Union or its satellites, individuals who by no stretch of the imagination qualify as political refugees. Similarly, for the political propaganda effect, the administration in 1980 enacted special legislation to enable the Marielitos, most of whom did not fit the test of fleeing persecution, to stay. A torrent of protest from civil rights groups indignant at the underlying racism forced the administration at that time to extend to a small group of Haitians the benefits of the law passed for the Cubans. The vast majority of Haitians and all the Central Americans, nevertheless, have continued to be discriminated against.

What this meant in 1980 was spelled out by federal judge James Lawrence King in his ruling in *Haitian Refugee Center v. Civiletti*. After hearing fifty-five witnesses and reviewing thousands of pages of exhibits, he found as follows:

The manner in which INS treated the more than 4,000 Haitian plaintiffs violated the Constitution, the immigration statutes, international agreements, INS regulations and INS operating procedures. It must stop.... The procedure to which Haitians were subjected is roughly equivalent of requiring a criminal defendant to concede his guilt before providing him any constitutional or statutory rights. ... Those Haitians who came to the United States seeking freedom and justice did not find it. Instead, they were confronted with an Immigration and Naturalization Service determined to deport them. The decision was made among high INS officials to expel Haitians, despite whatever claims to asylum individual Haitians might have. A program was set up to accomplish this goal. The program resulted in wholesale violations of due process. ... This program, in its planning and its execution, is offensive to every notion of constitutional due process and equal protection.[3]

Treatment of Central Americans at that time was no different. The INS, in the words of Antonio H. Rodríguez, director of the Los Angeles Center of Law and Justice, is the most arbitrary and openly racist policy body in the United States. "Its job is to arrest and deport as rapidly as possible, without regard to human or constitutional rights, such as the right to be represented by a lawyer, [the right to] a deportation hearing or [to] political asylum."[4]

The situation has become progressively worse since the start of the Reagan administration in 1981. In the words of a September 1981 Mission of the UN High Commissioner for Refugees (UNHCR) charged with monitoring the INS "asylum processing of

Salvadoran illegal immigrants": "It is therefore fair to conclude that this is a systematic practice designed to forcibly return Salvadorans irrespective of the merits of the asylum claims."[5] A suit filed in November 1981 by the National Center for Immigrants' Rights (NCIR) in the United States District Court, Central District of California, describes the experience of Crosby Wilfredo Orantes Hernández, who fled El Salvador after he had been beaten by the National Guard, his mother had her face smashed with a rifle, and two uncles had been carried off and later found dead with their heads mutilated and their sexual organs cut off. He arrived in the United States to become again—in the words of the brief—"a victim of violence and lawlessness."[6] In Culver City, California, an INS agent grabbed his arm as he left a bus and twisted it behind his back, and a second agent pistol-whipped him while the first held him, causing him to bleed profusely from mouth and nose. For days, agents tried to persuade him to sign "voluntary departure," even waking him at 3:00 A.M. and giving him coffee, apparently to deprive him of adequate sleep. He was never advised of his right to consult with counsel, of the availability of free legal services, of his right to a deportation hearing, or his right to apply for political asylum. Only after he was finally moved to El Centro was he able to phone a friend who arranged for a lawyer. He had received no medical attention for the injuries suffered at the time of his arrest.

In its Findings of Fact and Conclusions of Law in the Orantes Hernández suit, issued in June 1982, the U.S. District Court, Central District of California, took judicial notice of "grave conditions" existing in El Salvador.[7] It stated that "descriptions of unexplained disappearances, random violence, and retaliatory torture are corroborated by the findings of the President and the Department of State." The court stated that the "pervasive and arbitrary violence in El Salvador has been amply documented by international human rights organizations." Based on all the evidence submitted by NCIR, "the Court believes that it can take judicial notice of the following facts without having to second guess the Executive Branch's analysis of events in El Salvador, as feared by defendants: (1) El Salvador is currently in the midst of a widespread civil war; (2) the continuing military actions by both government and insurgent forces create a substantial danger of violence to civilians residing in El Salvador; and (3) Government forces . . . have been responsible for political persecution and human rights violations in the form of unexplained disappearances, arbitrary arrest, torture and murder."

Concerning the coerced signing of voluntary departure agreements, the court noted that "for many Salvadorans the decision to enter the United States is one born of desperation." Yet, "the hope and expectations which [these refugees] bring to the United States prove to be short-lived." The record before the court "indicates that the widespread acceptance of voluntary departure is due in large part to the coercive effect of the practices and procedures employed by the INS and the unfamiliarity of most Salvadorans with their rights under the immigration laws."

The process of securing a voluntary departure agreement "begins with the initial, sometimes abusive, contact between the INS agent and the apprehended Salvadoran." Following their arrest, Salvadorans are customarily taken to INS detention facilities for "processing." The evidence "before the court discloses a variety of techniques used by INS agents to obtain consent to voluntary departure, ranging from subtle persuasion to outright threats and misrepresentation." Further, "on this record it appears that Salvadorans are rarely given any notice of the existence of asylum procedures and [the INS lawyers] argue (before this Court) that such notice is not required." Plaintiffs who had specifically requested the opportunity to apply for political asylum have been "told that asylum was not available."

Salvadoran refugees "often are not allowed to consult with counsel until after they have consented to voluntary departure." Even those Salvadorans fortunate enough to secure legal representation "may be unable to avoid voluntary departure." INS's present practice "is to refuse to recognize the authority of counsel to stop the removal process until a formal notice of representation [form G–28] is filed." Yet "the record indicates that Salvadorans are frequently arrested, deposited in waiting rooms, interrogated, put onto buses, and flown back to El Salvador all in a matter of hours." Because of the rapidity of this process,

it is often physically impossible for counsel to locate their client and file the form G–28 before the client is removed from the country.

The record in this case indicates that the mistreatment of Salvadorans is not limited to any particular geographic area or to the conduct of a few INS agents. . . . [The] sheer volume of evidence before the Court and the similarity of the experiences therein belie the contention by defendants that plaintiff's claims center on isolated incidents of misconduct. . . . [The] Court concludes that INS agents routinely give incomplete, misleading, and even false advice to Salvadorans regarding their legal rights.

The few Salvadorans who resist coercion to waive their rights and instead apply for political asylum are forced to remain in the custody of INS detention centers while awaiting processing of their political asylum applications. "The record substantiate[s] plaintiff's charges of poor treatment and continued denial of legal information." The evidence convinced the court that "Salvadorans incarcerated in the INS facilities in Pasadena, Los Angeles, Chula Vista and El Centro are prohibited from receiving or possessing any written materials, with the exception of the New Testament of the Bible." The court found that "packets of written materials explaining the legal rights of aliens are routinely confiscated."

Incarcerated Salvadoran refugees "may receive visitors only during limited hours." These refugees "also experience great difficulty in obtaining access to telephones at these facilities."

On a nationwide basis, "defendants have adopted a policy that paralegals working under the supervision of counsel may not interview detainees unless the attorney is present." This policy severely hampered the ability of attorneys to provide legal services. In addition to limiting access to legal information and counsel, "defendants' current guidelines allow Salvadoran detainees to be placed in solitary confinement without notice or an opportunity to be heard."

Attorney Linton Joaquín of Los Angeles has summed up the common techniques used by the INS to deny Salvadorans access to attorneys and to deprive them of the right to apply for political asylum. After interviewing one of his clients, Joaquín gave him a packet of written materials explaining his legal rights: "At this point, one of the immigration agents called out, 'Let me see that,' and took the packet from my client. An agent named J. L. Hammer looked over the packet and stated, 'This is political propaganda.' My client was not allowed to have the packet. The packet consisted of a description of rights under the immigration laws and procedures for exercising these rights."[8]

Detainees are seldom informed on detention of the right to counsel, or of the right to apply for political asylum. Usually they are immediately ordered to sign a form, which is often misrepresented as simply a formality related to their detention, when in fact it is a voluntary departure form authorizing the INS to ship them back to their country of origin without further investigation. Refusal to sign brings threats that they will be jailed indefinitely if they cannot pay $5,000 bail and that in the end they will be deported anyway.

Access to the single phone at the Los Angeles processing center in the federal building is severely limited. Detainees arrested in the morning usually cannot get to the phone before afternoon. If they have unwittingly signed the voluntary departure form, this leaves little time for revoking it after consultation with an attorney, and, in fact, many are shipped back to El Salvador the same day, while the revocation papers are still being processed. Detainees are at times physically prevented access to phones.

Attorney Marc Van Der Hout of the National Lawyers Guild National Immigration Project confirms this evaluation. In a sworn statement he states that he has seen:

A pattern of practice develop regarding INS treatment of Salvadorans which has substantially deviated from past treatment of citizens from other countries encountered by INS. In my opinion, there has been a concerted effort on the part of INS officials to attempt to expedite the departure of Salvadorans in whatever manner possible. . . . The consistent pattern that I have observed is the practice of INS officials trying to coerce the Salvadorans into signing form I–274, to "voluntarily" leave the United States without asserting their right to a deportation hearing where they could apply for political asylum. Threats, giving of false information as to the political asylum process and other means are used in an attempt to coerce individuals into signing I–274. Moreover, extraordinarily high bails have been set in Salvadoran cases in the hope that the individual will give up his/her right to a deportation hearing rather than remain incarcerated for many months. . . . Moreover, the manner in which the State Department Bureau of Human Rights and Humanitarian Affairs has responded to the requests for political asylum has evidenced a disregard for the facts of the individual cases and resulted in a *pro forma* recommendation for denial of the asylum application.[9]

The "extraordinarily high bails" are something that we of the Task Force on Central America of the Tucson Ecumenical Council can confirm from our own experience. The law is clearly established that bonds in deportation hearings are intended to ensure the appearance of the alien and must not be punitive. When the Task Force began in 1980 to work with Central American refugees, practice usually conformed to the law. If we took an applicant for asylum to the INS office, generally he or she was released into our custody without posting a bond. The Reagan administration changed all that. Bonds were set at $100, then $250, $1,000, and finally, often $3,500 or more. We managed to raise between half a million and a million dollars in cash and collateral, but there was no way we could beat the INS at its own game. This vindictive escalation of bonds played a large part in our decision to start the sanctuary movement.

Conditions in the holding centers for those unable to raise bail money are simply scandalous. These centers are located in remote areas far from legal and paralegal services. It required federal court action to enable representatives of the TEC Task Force to interview refugees at El Centro who had asked help in filing asylum petitions. We soon discovered why the INS had wanted to keep us out as they kept reporters and photographers out.

Detainees told of guards yelling at them to hurry as they ate food that was inadequate in quantity and often inedible. If they did not obey they were liable to be put into solitary confinement. The detainees had to remain locked in a corral inside the barracks compound in which they were housed from 6:00 A.M. until 8:00 P.M. It had no greenery, and a couple of open-sided lean-tos provided shade for only a fraction of the three hundred to four hundred men. During the long summer most had to stand, sit, or lie on the ground under a blazing sun that regularly raised the temperature to between 110 and 120 degrees. Even those lucky enough to find shade seldom stayed there long, because of the swarms of flies. Barracks were not heated in the winter, when the temperature at night dropped into the forties.

There was neither a doctor nor a nurse at the camp, although a very high proportion of the detainees had obvious health problems resulting from inadequate nutrition in their homeland and the hardship of travel to the United States. One man had fallen while on kitchen duty and injured his right arm. He could not bend his elbow and was obviously in great pain. The guards had refused to treat him or even give him a pain reliever, and he had improvised a bandage from a piece of rag to help ease the pain. Our protests succeeded two days later in having him taken, in handcuffs, to a doctor who gave him some pills but failed to diagnose the injury. Several days later, when we bonded him out, it was established that his arm was broken.

Similar conditions characterize other holding centers. The detainees have fewer rights and less access to redress for violations of their rights than prisoners serving sentences for major crimes. The clear objective is to make life so intolerable for the Central Americans that they will sign "voluntary departure" statements, after which they can be shipped back to their country of origin. After an extensive survey in the Southwest of the United States, representatives of the Washington Liaison Office of the UN High Commissioner for Refugees reported that there appeared to be "a systematic practice designed to secure the return of Salvadorans, irrespective of their rights." In addition, the UN High Commissioner twice wrote the U.S. government warning that it may be in violation of international law and endangering thousand of lives with its deportation procedures.

A further pressure on Central Americans has been introduced by the Reagan administration. Previously, those released from detention centers on bond were authorized to work while awaiting determination of their application for asylum. Such authorization is no longer given, so that refugees cannot get Social Security cards, without which many firms will not employ them. This leaves them subject to exploitation in marginal activities on the edge of the labor force. Recently some INS officials are making it a specific condition of the bond that the refugee is not to take paid employment. That means that if he or she is found working, the bond is subject to forfeiture.

Finally, some words about the INS administrative courts: Under federal regulations, a refugee who has not been served with an order to show cause (the initiation of formal deportation proceedings) is entitled to have his or her application for political asylum adjudicated by an INS district director. In defiance of these regulations, the INS policy and practice with Central Americans is to prevent district directors from considering such requests for asylum, thus denying a remedy that is potentially of benefit to many applicants.

Instead, all applicants are subjected to deportation proceedings. Unlike the nonadversarial hearings before a district director, these are strictly adversary proceedings. The immigration judge (who is an INS employee) frequently joins the INS attorney in trying to confuse applicants who do not understand legal procedures into admitting that they are really economic and not political refugees. If the applicant has an attorney this process is interrupted and an elaborate form detailing the grounds for claiming asylum is submitted to the State Department. The department is obligated to evaluate the concrete facts of each application and give an advisory opinion for or against the granting of asylum. Their recommendation goes back to the INS district director, who may accept or reject the asylum application.

Instead of evaluating the concrete facts of each application, the State Department usually responds with a form denial. There are cases on record in which the denial was dated before the application for review had even reached the State Department.

The INS courts cooperate in the overall strategy to curtail or deny the rights of the applicants. Having participated in many deportation hearings as an expert witness in Tucson, Phoenix, and El Centro, I can testify that most hearings do not meet the basic standards of law and equity. The judge almost invariably operates as a second prosecuting attorney. Moreover, the information the refugee would need to give to substantiate a claim for asylum is often such as to jeopardize relatives still in El Salvador or Guatemala. Not only is there no guarantee that such information will not be given to the claimant's government, but it has been established that in one instance inaccurate information was transmitted that led to the arrest and harassment of an innocent woman. In consequence, many refugees are afraid to report facts that would help their claim. Another catch-22 is that evidence needed to support a claim can be and is used by the judge to rule the claimant an immoral person and excludable as such. For example, a former member of the Salvadoran-Guatemalan defense forces, in order to substantiate his claim that he has a reasonable fear of being killed if returned, may have to testify that for a time he had carried out acts of torture or killings at the command of his superior officer, but finally decided that he could not conscientiously continue to do this. His admission of having for a time performed acts in violation of human rights may be used to rule that he is an immoral person. This is forcing the individual to incriminate him- or herself, something clearly contrary to our legal tradition and to equity.

Finally, regardless of the evidence, the INS judge almost invariably rules against the Central American. The most recent example of this is found in a ruling of the Ninth Circuit Federal Court in December 1984, "The Board's conclusion that the threat against Bolanos's life was insufficient simply becuase it was representative of the general level of violence in El Salvador constitutes a clear error of law," the judges said. "We are mystified by the Board's ability to turn logic on its head. . . . Interpreting the 'objective evidence' requirement in the manner suggested by the immigration judge would erect a virtually insuperable barrier to the attainment of refugee status."[10]

As part of a general policy of expansion of the powers of the executive branch of government, the Reagan administration has been promoting major changes in immigration law (the Simpson-Mazzoli bill). One provision it seeks would exclude most appeals to the federal courts from the decisions of the INS administrative judges. Given the history of political manipulation of the INS courts, such a change would be disastrous for Haitians and Central Americans today, and for God-knows-which asylum seekers tomorrow. It would also represent a further threat to the rights of all of us, rights already weakened by the progressive encroachment of the executive into the areas allocated to the legislature and the judiciary by the U.S. Constitution.

Given the facts, I would suggest that all who are concerned for the rights, including the right to life, of refugees, should give high priority to a campaign for congressional hearings on the Immigration and Naturalization Service. Its abuses are a challenge to our Judeo-Christian values and to our national identity. Government lawlessness, far more than technically illegal border crossing, undermines the fabric of respect for the law that maintains our social order.

NOTES

1. Michael Maggio, "Shifting Sands of U.S. Immigration Policy Trap Salvadoran Refugees," *Los Angeles Times* (13 July 1980), part V, p. 1.

2. *Asylum Adjudications: An Evolving Concept and Responsibility for the Immigration and Naturalization Service* (Washington, D.C.: Immigration and Naturalization Service, June 1982), p. 59.
3. *Haitian Refugee Center v. Civiletti*, 503 E. Supp. 442 (1980), p. 452 and p. 520 ff.
4. Rafael Prieto Zartha, "No se da una huelga de hambre de salvadoreños, afirma el Director de Inmigración" (There is no hunger strike of Salvadorans, immigration director asserts), *La Opinión* (8 January 1981), p. 3.
5. Congressional Record, Senate, S 826, 11 February 1982.
6. *Immigration Law Bulletin*, National Center for Immigrants' Rights, Inc. 1544 West 8th Street, Los Angeles, 90017, vol. 3, no. 5 (Spring 1985), pp. 3 ff.
7. Circular to Gary MacEoin from National Center for Immigrants' Rights, Los Angeles, March 1982.
8. Personal letter from Linton Joaquín to Gary MacEoin, March 1982.
9. Full text of affidavit in *No Promised Land*, by Gary MacEoin and Nivita Riley (Boston: Oxfam America, 1982), pp. 73–77.
10. *Bolanos-Hernández v. The Immigration and Naturalization Service*, 749 F. 2d 1216 (9th cir., 1984), p. 1323.

Response by William L. Wipfler

Senator DeConcini's bill to grant temporary asylum to Central Americans will have an effect on the sanctuary movement. The bill would change the nature of the movement but would not change one of its purposes. That purpose is to continue to make clear the nature of the results of the kind of engagement the United States has practiced in Central America. This is a very important issue and one that must be kept alive regardless of whether or not there is a formal sanctuary movement. In a way, the DeConcini-Moakley bill is one that provides a temporary sanctuary, in a legal sense, to Salvadorans who are here.

However, an aspect of the best message of refugees in public sanctuary is the constant reminder that they are refugees, many of them because of U.S. foreign policy. A granting of extended voluntary departure, which you hear many speak of, simply means that persons present in the United States are granted a stay and will be allowed to continue here until the conditions that caused their departure from their country have changed and they can safely return. Since they go back voluntarily, they are allowed to remain voluntarily. Once the bill is passed and they are allowed to stay, the sanctuary movement as such is altered. One of the reasons for sanctuary, however, is not changed, since the bill will not change U.S. policy in Central America.

CHAPTER 14

THE INTERNATIONAL
STRUGGLE FOR HUMAN RIGHTS
Marshall T. Meyer

In 1984 I returned to the United States after twenty-five years in Argentina. In my last days there, as a member of the Presidential Commission, we presented to Dr. Raul Alfonsin, president of Argentina, the final report on over ten thousand disappeared Argentinians. When in September 1984 we finally turned the list in to Dr. Alfonsin, our computer registered a total of about 9,200. But we knew full well that there were still parents who were afraid to turn in the name of their child, or children afraid to turn in the name of their parent, because they thought that either they might still find them alive, or that by turning in a name they themselves might be in danger.

One dines rather late in Buenos Aires, 9:30 or 10:00, and frequently you find yourself sitting around waiting for your son or daughter to come back from university or from studying for high school, or for your married child and spouse to come over for dinner; they may be an hour or two late. Well, given Argentinian punctuality, it is within the realm of possibility to be an hour late, even two hours late. But finally, it's three hours late, and there's a knock on the door or the door is blown apart with a blast of machine gun fire. Ten men, and this time men, not women, come into your apartment, give your wife a crack on her head with the butt of a machine gun that knocks her out and leaves a mass of her blood on the wall. You are cracked on the head and hooded. You hear them go into your wife's or your child's bedroom, and the entire bedroom is destroyed. Then you hear some gorillas scream out: "Here's a subversive book, here's a book by Freud, here's one by Jung, here's one by Marx." I might add that in all of the years that I went to prisons visiting the prisoners in Argentina, the Bible was considered the primary subversive text, especially if it contained the original Hebrew. I could not get a Bible or a prayer book into any prison. It was considered totally subversive literature by those who always spoke in terms reminiscent of Julius Caesar. The rallying point of the military junta was, "We are fighting in the name of Christianity and Western values."

The more you heard the words, "Western values," "Christianity," and things like that from the mouths of these devils, the more you became aware of what was going on. And finally your parent, son, or daughter would come home, frequently showing signs of a beating or apparent cruel treatment. If you were lucky, when he or she walked in the door, he or she was killed in front of your eyes. Because if not, and you did not have a cadaver to bury, six or seven years later you were still looking for a cadaver, and you could still not accept the fact that the person was taken away and killed.

In the morning you went to the police and you went to the Ministry of Interior and you went to the army and the navy and the air force, and they all told you that it was your imagination, that nothing happened in your home the previous night. Frequently, the next day a truck pulled up and stripped your apartment of everything it contained.

Above all, you wanted to know, when the blast of the machine gun went off, what the response was of the people who were living in the apartment on the right. They had been living there as your neighbors for twenty years. Did anybody come in and ask, "What's the noise?" The whole street down below was blocked with Ford Falcons without license plates.

Nobody stopped. Your concierge didn't ask you anything, nor did the people above or the people below. The final blow was when you picked up your telephone and you spoke to your brother or your sister, asking, "What shall I do? Miguel is not coming home, he hasn't come home." They deny the whole thing, saying: "You know I love you, you know I love Miguel, but I've got to be careful. I have my own children." What have I learned in Argentina under the most harrowing experiences of my life? Those who persecute, those who torture, those who kill, count on your silence. It is their greatest asset. Our becoming accomplices by silence and by allowing fear to paralyze us is what makes us not at all useful as Jews or Christians or human beings, but makes us robots for those who would control our lives.

I returned to the United States from Argentina, which has gone through a miraculous transformation from military fascist dictatorship to democracy, without civil war. In late 1984 I went back to Argentina for the Jewish high holidays and spoke at a gathering for human rights that attracted a fervent multitude, because the people had come out of the most savage period of Argentinian history, a period when human life was worth practically nothing. When now I hear the learned and passionate spokespersons of the sanctuary movement and I read the daily newspaper, I do not know to what country I have returned. I am in deep cultural shock. What is happening here is too reminiscent of the terror I knew in Argentina.

From 24 March 1976 until 10 December 1983, whenever I wanted the government to know exactly what I was doing, and when I wanted to get a message through to them, I picked up the telephone and called any one of my friends, because my telephone and my friends' telephones were always tapped. To think that in the United States of America, in churches and in synagogues, there are people taping proceedings and meetings brings me back to my synagogue in Buenos Aires under a fascist military dictatorship, when I could see people sitting in the synagogue amongst the twelve hundred people every Friday night turning their tape recorders on, knowing full well that it would all be transcribed and turned over to the government Monday morning. I feel a deep pain, a deep shame. One thing I say to our brothers and sisters from Central America is that *we*, not *they*, are the refugees.

I was on a fact-finding mission to Nicaragua this summer, and I found thousands of young Americans working with their Nicaraguan brothers and sisters. I saw their fear, and I entered into profound discussions with the governing junta in Managua about the possibilities of an American invasion.

When I returned from Argentina I went to the State Department and the White House. I tried to get the message across that from 1976 to 1983, the embassy of the United States of America was the place most sought out by those individuals whose lives were in danger under the Argentinian military dictatorship. I remember taking various taxis in Buenos Aires to meet with Patricia Derian, under-secretary of state for human rights, who was visiting Argentina. I remember with what enormous respect the families of the *desaparecidos* came to the American embassy. I remember the extraordinary work of Tex Harris. There they saw the possibility of life and liberty and the pursuit of happiness, and all of these very, very beautiful words that evidently have no meaning to the people who currently occupy the same buildings and houses where those same words were penned.

And if I was in culture shock then, I'm trembling now. Perhaps the only thing that gives me the strength to speak is the fact that I speak in a synagogue, which could easily be a church. Because herein is not only the brotherhood of faith, but people sitting here with their hearts as well as their bodies. Herein is also the future as well as those pages of the past that we must capture once again, those pages of the past that made the United States a country in which we wanted our children to live.

I cannot defend any part of our government's policy. I can give you a few figures. According to demographic prognoses, in fifteen years (barring a cataclysmic apocalypse of nuclear proportions in which there will be no refugees because there will be no world because there will be no people), there will be 260 million Americans. I don't know what kind of world, if any at all, we will have in the twenty-first century. When I think about the future, I think that perhaps the most important thing I could say is to quote my great teacher, Abraham Joshua Heschel, who said at the peak of the Vietnam War: "We are not all guilty, but we are all responsible." All of us should be arraigned, and I think that we should take our places together with our brothers and sisters who have been indicted and add our names and say to the government: "You want more than sixteen? Here are another couple of million, arrest all of us." I would like to make that suggestion a genuine and sincere motion.

I think that we should present to Washington a few million signatures of people who are ready to be arrested because we are not going to sacrifice to the modern Molech or any of the other baalim or the idols of the Caesars who want to govern the most recondite parts of our souls. The only thing that is really worth taking care of for the future is the purity of our conscience. I would suggest also, that, since the United States of America is a signatory of the Organization of American States, that the Inter-American Court of Human Rights receive a petition signed by millions of Americans asking the court to take up this subject. I think it is high time that Mr. Reagan be called upon to openly state that he no longer recognizes the World Court in the Hague and he no longer recognizes the Inter-American Court in Costa Rica; that is to say, he recognizes no court and no law.

I frequently ask myself, as a Jew, as a rabbi, who was only twelve years of age in 1942: where was American Jewry in 1942 and 1943 when the first clips came through of Auschwitz and Dachau? Why weren't there at least three million American Jews at the Washington Mall on a starvation diet refusing a drop of water until the railroad tracks to Dachau or Auschwitz were bombed?

I ask today that all of us, Christians and Jews, unite. If we cannot unite over sanctuary then there is no future for anything or anybody. We should go to Washington several million strong and really make our voices heard. Is this our country, or is it not our country? For those of the CIA and the FBI who spy on us, I've met you before, I greet you again. And, I feel very sorry for you. I feel very sorry for all infected minds who cannot distinguish any longer the basic difference between an animal and a human being: human powers of reason to determine what is right and what is wrong.

I know full well that the death squads are trained by the CIA. This is common knowledge. We know the CIA trains the contras in Honduras. And, with regard to the demographic projection mentioned earlier, in fifteen years, there will probably be some 260 million North Americans, and some 35–40 million Canadians, but south of the Rio Grande there will be some 500 million Latin Americans.

Already, 62 percent of the population in the primary and secondary schools in Los Angeles today is Latino. There is one common denominator among most Latin Americans. They don't understand us; they dislike us intensely, and for the right reasons. We have dealt with them as our "backyard." How would you like it if Canada treated the United States as its backyard and carried a big stick and played banana republic with us?

The Jewish challenge is similar to what Professor McAfee Brown has said about the Christian challenge. I hear a number of Jews saying, "How many Guatemalans are Jews? They're Roman Catholics. How many Salvadorans are Jews? Very few." If we ignore this mass murder, we will participate in this great catastrophe in the eyes of the living God as understood in our tradition and in the Torah. There is only one God of all people, and whether we like it or not, the rhetorical question that rings out as a result of the first dialogue between the brothers Cain and Abel is a lesson for us.

It is registered that they spoke to each other. They were not Jews, they were just human beings; there were no Jews, there were no Hebrews. Cain kills Abel. "Where is Abel, your brother?" God calls out in Hebrew. (At least so it is registered in the Hebrew Bible. I do not think God only speaks Hebrew. If he does, he's not God.) At any rate, the answer is, of course, the answer of humanity for the last four thousand years: "Am I my brother's keeper?" And the answer is, whether we like it or not: "Yes." We are our brother's keeper. It is not an easy thing to be, and most people shy away from it. What have we got to do with most of the other people on this earth? Each one of you has your own package of difficulties (which is a very good translation from the Yiddish); everybody has his or her own share.

But the simple fact is that *your* problems ultimately are *my* problems, especially when your problem is one of hunger or persecution. "When they came after the black, I wasn't worried, I'm not black. When they came after the Jew, I wasn't worried, I wasn't a Jew. When they came after me, it was too late." We are our brothers' keepers, all of us, each and every one of us.

And the concept of sanctuary, with a little bit of theology, comes from the word *sanctus*. In the sixth chapter of the Book of Isaiah, in the Revelation of God it says *Kadosh, Kadosh, Kadosh*, which is *Sanctus, Sanctus, Sanctus*. What is holy, what is *hekdesh* in Hebrew? *Hekdesh* is that which is set apart for God. Let there be no silence in the synagogues, nor the churches, nor in our hearts and actions.

Human beings have been set apart to serve God, and the cardinal principle of Christianity, which it has learned from Judaism, which has been taught by the theophany to Isaiah, is the sanctity of life. And that is why there is a sanctuary movement. It exists not only to fight against the powers of evil and idolatry but to celebrate the sanctity of life and to help people to live in spite of persecution, to give them the faith and the courage to confront what is practically destroying the whole of Central America.

We Jews and Christians can understand the sanctity of life. Let us be brothers and sisters, responsible one for another, and let us celebrate life and its sanctuary and its sanctity, and if needs be, we will celebrate in prison.

CHAPTER 15

THE TRADITIONS AND CULTURE OF THE MAYAN-QUICHÉ PEOPLE

Felipe Ixcot Jalben

My name is Felipe Ixcot Jalben. I am from the province of Quezaltenango. I speak the language Mam, one of the twenty-two Mayan languages spoken in present-day Guatemala. I am an Indian *campesino* and Christian of conscience. I would like you to know a little of Guatemala as I know it. I will begin by describing some of the history of the area of Quezaltenango from which my family and I come.

Before the Spanish invasion of our country, the city of Quezaltenango was known by the indigenous name Xe Lajuj Noj. The word *xe* means "under," *lajuj*, "ten," *noj*, "powers." "Under the ten powers" refers to the ten Mayan altars, one on each of the ten hills that surround the city of Quezaltenango. It is upon these altars that our people worshiped God as manifested as the God of Corn, God of Wind, God of Rain, and God of the Moon. It is here they would go to ask permission of Mother Earth to cut into her breast in order to plant their corn.

In February 1524 the conqueror Pedro de Alvarado, together with his criminal band of mercenaries, attacked the indigenous people of the western part of the country, the area from which my family and I come. On the banks of the River Samalá the Spanish and the Indian people confronted each other in a bloody battle. Our ancestors had never met an army trained for war as were the Spanish. The Spanish conquered and massacred our people, not because they were militarily superior but because they encountered a people who were simply not warlike. The Spanish had come to kill and brought different forms of arms to do this.

It was there on the banks of the River Samalá that our great national hero Tecún Umán was killed. The story passed on to us is that our people renamed this river Xe Quijel, "River of Blood," because the river was colored red from the blood of our massacred people. And the story goes on to say that when our hero Tecún Umán fell dying on the ground, a bird called the quetzal was flying overhead and landed on the palpitating breast of Tecún Umán, and they both died together. The death of the quetzal bird symbolizes the death of "freedom" for the indigenous people and the beginning of the over-shadowing clouds of repression. It is said that the quetzal bird is the spirit *(nahual)* of Tecún Umán, because this bird dies immediately in captivity.

This all happened in the municipality of Olintepeque, very close to the city of Xe Lajuj Noj. After this, the Spanish removed the name of the city and baptized it "Quezaltenango," taken from the quetzal bird. "Quetzal" is also the name of the national money of Guatemala.

The people of the city of Quezaltenango speak the Quiché language, and the women wear a multicolored and distinctive native dress. In the province of Quezaltenango there are twenty-four municipalities, ten of which speak the Quiché language, thirteen, Mam, and the remaining one, only Spanish and no indigenous language. I have begun to tell you only a little about who we are as the Mayan Indians of Guatemala. I wish I could tell you more about the life of my people, but space does not allow this. So I will continue only outlining the present-day situation.

Because of the high percentage of Guatemalans who can be characterized as indigenous people, or Indians, Guatemala is considered one of the six indigenous countries in Latin America. Of all these Indians, the Mayan-Quiché people from Guatemala have left the richest mythology. The book of the Popol Vuh describes their world-view. The Popol Vuh is like a Mayan Bible, the national book of the Mayan-Quiché people. Its rough, strange eloquence and poetic originality make it one of the most valuable relics of Indian thought.

Because the Spaniards destroyed the records and many of the material structures of my Mayan ancestors, their origins remain a mystery. Most scholars now agree, however, that the Mayan civilization flourished from 1500 B.C. up to about A.D. 1500. The classical period runs from A.D. 300 to 900. Some surviving stories say that the

Aztecs called all the land south of Mexico or south of the Yucatan Quauhtlemallan. The word *quauhtlemallan* means "mountainous land" and "fertile land," and from it came the Spanish name, Guatemala.

The Mayans were not backward people as some of our oppressors say. Materially they were highly advanced. Even though they were isolated from the rest of the world, what remains of their achievements reveals their native capacities or abilities. You can look, for instance, at their architecture and the buildings of the great temples that still stand, like Tikal, Petén-Itzá, Uaxactún, Piedras Negras, Zaculeu, and many others. The Mayans were great astronomers; they measured the movements of the stars exactly. They had an amazing calendar, extraordinarily accurate. They had great artistic and poetic abilities.

Their ruler or leader was called the principal lord. Next to him were the wise men and the priests; the priests had both political and religious power. Beyond that, we know little about the social organization of our ancestors. Much study remains to be done. We do know, however, that there were other groups who were also very much respected. And we know that there was neither slavery nor exploitation.

It is impossible for us to imagine how the Mayan people acquired all their knowledge, especially when we remember that they did not know the wheel or metal and were also isolated from the rest of the world. It is amazing to realize how many organized structures existed. Some were dedicated to agriculture, others to weaving, ceramics, business, religion, architecture, painting and writing, other artisanships, and the study of mathematics, the stars, literature, music, and dance. We also know from the few stories that survive that Mayans did not know what hunger was. We even think that they were better fed than the Europeans. What then did the conquest bring for us, the indigenous people? It brought us the terror of the destruction of a culture, of a people, and of a social organization. It was also the first step in the imposition of a system of exploitation and humiliation that persists to our day and under which we still live and suffer.

Mayan society had never before known a system of abuses, exploitation, or humiliation like that introduced by the Spaniards. My ancestors were treated worse than beasts of burden. They were marked with iron like cattle. They were forced to work at hard labor so that the criminal invaders could be fed. In spite of this beastly treatment, the Spaniards were not able to destroy all of us. Much of the culture we still celebrate and hold we have inherited from our Mayan ancestors. The Mayans did not end. We are the continuation of our Mayan forebears. Just the little we have learned about them gives us a hint of their greatness. Their masterworks were not made only by privileged individuals; they are the product of the common people, the product of a great culture with a well-developed art, religion, and science.

Today in Guatemala 61 percent of us are indigenous people or Indians. There are twenty-two Mayan languages and 288 different forms of dress in Guatemala. Our main staples are corn, wheat, beans, wild plants, and roots or tubers like potatoes. The tun and chirimilla (drum and flute) constitute our original, unique autochthonous music. The musical notes of our marimba make us immediately identifiable anywhere in the world.

When the Spaniards came, our ancestors struggled not to lose their lives, their customs, their culture. The Spaniards encountered great opposition and bitter combat. The Mayans came down from the mountains where they lived to the valleys where the Spaniards were gathered. They made big traps, big holes with very sharp pieces of wood. When the horses and the Spaniards fell into them, they would die there. They also attacked the Spaniards with arrows and spears.

The history and struggle of our people is not a struggle provoked by Cuba or Russia or any other outside power. What we are doing is following the example of our ancestors. Our struggle is based on the values of our ancestors, the Mayans. I want to make it perfectly clear to this noble people of North America that we are not giving ourselves, selling ourselves, lending ourselves to the interests of the Russians or the Cubans or any other people, but that we are inspired by our own ancestors to defend our lands and customs, our lives and culture.

Our tradition says we were formed out of corn. But today the government of Guatemala does not allow us anymore to plant corn, which means that they are killing us directly because—as the Popol

Vuh tells us—we are made of corn. Why do they not let us plant corn? Why are they stealing our land? There are two reasons. One is that they want to give that land to the wealthy oligarchs. The other is that they want to starve us in order to make us subservient to those wealthy oppressors. Our culture is sustained by the land, our culture is sustained by the corn, and if they take our land away from us they take away from us our culture and our very life.

Guatemala is a very rich country. But all this richness is for the great monopolists in Guatemala. We have cotton, for instance, sugar, and cacao. We export beef. We also have oil, although we do not know how much or where it goes. That is why we have a "scorched earth" policy in the three northern provinces. That is where the nucleus of oil is. But all that land belonged to our ancestors for centuries, as did the land of other linguistic groups belong to theirs. Now they want to expel all of us so that they can own that land. That is the reason for the "scorched earth" plan against the natives.

It is not only wealthy people from Guatemala, however, who are oppressing us. They are in alliance also with wealthy families and people from the United States and also from Israel. That is why now they have moved into this more sophisticated way of destroying us under President Mejía Víctores. They are still trying to subdue the natives, just as the Spaniards subdued our ancestors. They have established Vietnam-style encampments to subdue us. And they don't allow us to plant corn, under the excuse that we are feeding the guerrillas. We are only permitted to plant export products such as capers and raspberries. These products are sent to the United States; then, as a reward, the United States sends back corn to be distributed by the military in a rationed way.

I noted earlier that I am a *campesino* of Christian conscience and belief. I want to add that I was also a catechist, a lay leader in the church who led my sisters and brothers in reading the Bible and in discussing what it means to us in our struggle for liberation. I think this is a very important issue to clarify, because in Central America we Christians are often accused of being a branch of Marxism-Leninism. But that is not true. When we Christians begin to practice what we have learned from God and from the Lord, this is regarded as a crime against the system. In the town in which I was born, about 75 percent of the people are illiterate. At the national level—

and I'm speaking now only of the indigenous people, the Indians—88 percent of us are illiterate.

Now when Jesus went about doing good, we understand that he was telling us something about that situation. According to the Scriptures, Jesus restored the sick to health, gave sight to the blind, healed the man with the withered hand by the synagogue, and made the lame walk. We have to materialize these facts in our lives. For Guatemala we have, in fact, 88 percent of our people who cannot see, not because they were born that way but because they were made that way. These then are our Christs; they have a right to see, and they must be taught to read and write. This is Christianity, not Marxism.

Following the example of Christ who helped the lame to walk, we must help our people to walk and show them the path so that no one can tell them that this is not, or that the other is, the path they should follow. Also we learned that Jesus helped the mute people, the deaf-mute people; he taught them how to speak or made them speak. In Guatemala for four centuries we have not been able to speak, because we have been silenced by bullets. This will not continue for another four centuries. Therefore we, like Christ, must also teach our brothers and sisters to speak in the same way in which Christ taught them to speak. And this is the greatest crime that a Christian can commit in a country that is ruled by exploiters.

As a Christian I wanted to be side by side with my brothers and my sisters. The government of Guatemala saw that as a crime, and the government said, "This Felipe, we'll have to persecute and kill because he is with his people." From the time I was sixteen years old, before I married Elena, I was already working with my community. I taught the very little I had learned in school—all I had was four years in elementary school. The few seeds of knowledge that I had I could not just hold to myself. I had to share with my brothers and sisters. And this I continued to do. When I married Elena, there were two of us. I had another arm to continue passing on the bread of knowledge to my brothers and sisters who had need of it.

When we talk about malnutrition we should not only think about bread and tamales and tortillas but also about malnutrition of the brain, about lack of knowledge—lack of knowledge that comes not because people want to be that way but because they have been forced to be that way. That is why we have the classification of superior and inferior peoples. The monopolizers of power have even gone so far as to say that those who are clever or smart were born that way. This is a lie, because God created us equals, endowed us all equally. The difference lies in opportunity. That is why Guatemala is in the midst of this trouble now, so that we all may have opportunity, so that all of us may indeed be equal. That is what I did in Guatemala, and that is why they wanted to kill me.

My principles as a Christian are nonviolent, as are the principles of the people of Guatemala, 80 percent of whom are Christian. That is why the people of El Quiché wanted to dialogue with the government, so that they would stop stealing our land. But in Guatemala it is no longer possible to gain our freedom through dialogue. In consequence, we have to forge the solution ourselves with the support of the authentic Christians of the entire world.

Just as the people from El Quiché were met with mockery, so were the people from Huehuetenango when they made a pilgrimage to Guatemala City, a distance of some 250 kilometers, to demand better salaries. The people from El Quiché also went and tried to talk to the Congress, but they were not heard; and when they came out, one by one their leaders were kidnapped by people, American-looking, in automobiles with dark-tinted windows. The cars were American. It was after these events that they decided to take the embassy. They took the Spanish embassy in January 1980, and the answer of the powerful was to burn that embassy. The hope of the people was that the Spanish ambassador could be a mediator between the native people and the government of Guatemala. But the government did not want dialogue, so the government burned the embassy. Thirty-nine people died, burned inside the embassy. The dead were not only natives or Indians. There were also professionals, Ladinos, schoolteachers, and so on, most of them Christians. It was a clear demonstration that the government did not care who opposed them, whether they were professionals or not. Anyone in opposition was destroyed. There, in the burning of the Spanish embassy, the hope for dialogue was also burned. It died there, because it was then very obvious that the wealthy and the government reject any dialogue. I want this to be clearly understood. The people of Guatemala do not want war; war is being imposed on the people by the powerful in

Guatemala. And now that the people are really speaking out, now the powerful say it is Russia, it is Cuba, though, in fact, it was their own action that closed the door to dialogue.

Therefore, dear people and good sons and daughters of this country, through what I have shared with you, we have journeyed briefly to Guatemala. My hope is that all the discriminated against and exploited peoples of the world, all men and women workers, all true Christians and peoples of faith, may stand in solidarity with the rightful and authentic struggle of the indigenous and other exploited people of Guatemala.

To conclude, I would like to leave you with a saying that our Mayan ancestors taught us in the Popol Vuh. It says:

> Let us all rise up together;
> Let us call out to everyone!
> Let no one group among us
> be left behind the rest.

Thank you for listening to Guatemala!

Response by Marilyn Chilcote

Our enormous capacity as North Americans to feel superior comes in part, I suspect, from our failure to give ourselves the opportunity to know and appreciate the culture and the history, and hence to recognize the genuine personhood, of people from Central America. Felipe Ixcot Jalben, in consequence, poses a challenge for the whole sanctuary movement.

In our effort to aid our Mayan brothers and sisters, and those from the other cultures involved in the plight that causes them to find themselves in our midst, we must not continue the destruction and the obliteration of the heritage that they bring.

We must join, or at least not further impede, their struggle to preserve, not only their lives, but their customs, culture, and values. And we have scarcely begun to address the question of how we're going to do that here in our own setting.

Early on, the sanctuary movement recognized how difficult real solidarity is. We've had to ask ourselves, for instance, if solidarity is possible with people whose language we do not speak. Some of us at least speak Spanish, but now we must look beyond that. Is solidarity possible when we continue to live behind the separating barriers of our own wealth and privilege? The challenge demands more than constant self-correction on our part.

We are dependent in ways we never imagined before on the kind of mutuality that solidarity implies. We need the cleansing power of faithful dialogue. We need to pray for the peace that comes of relaxing our own defensive egos and becoming vulnerable to the truth of our new solidarity; I mean the oneness of human souls beloved of God. We are promised that, in this way, we will discover the profoundest blessings that life has to offer.

CHAPTER 16

LIVING WITH FAITH AND HOPE

Evaluation of sanctuary calls for views of people from different geographical and cultural backgrounds. In this chapter, refugees from Central America give a sense of what sanctuary means for them and how they would like to see it develop. Their comments also reflect their surprise at the fact that, while many Americans welcome them as friends, they are forced to live as criminals. With the exception of Marta Benavides, all of the refugees' names are fictitious. They fear that using their real names might cause suffering for their family members still in El Salvador or Guatemala.

What We as Refugees Feel About Sanctuary—Roberto

As a Salvadoran, I can attest that the history of all the peoples of Central America is a history of unending resistance. In the same way as the Mayans resisted in Guatemala, so did the Hondurans with Lempira, the Salvadorans with Atlacatl, the Nicaraguans with Nicarao, the Costa Ricans with Raca. We in Central America have inherited a long tradition of resistance against oppression and injustice, and this tradition is at the root of today's movement for social and political change in Central America. Since the Spanish came to Central America between 1520 and 1550, the resistance has been uninterrupted.

We are the survivors of five centuries of struggle, almost five hundred years of fighting against injustice, against a system implanted by the Spanish and that continues, with changes, to operate today. They imposed on us an economic structure in which a minority of the population—an elite—controls most of the economy, especially the land, which is vital to survival in agrarian countries.

Centuries have passed. The pressure on our people has continued, as has our resistance. Now we are in the twentieth century, but the same injustice continues. A small minority still controls the economy, supported by an army that dominates the political life of the country.

Our people do not want to live under this oppression, and that is why we are fighting. Since 1979, there has been a radical and important change in Central America. I can think of no more important historical change in the history of our people than the Nicaraguan revolution, which started building a new society in Central America. It gives hope to our countries, in terms of how we want to develop, how we want to base new societies on peace and justice.

In El Salvador, we are living a civil war that has produced sixty thousand deaths in five years. Every Salvadoran family has a history of fear because of this war. We have three thousand disappeared persons, persons who have been taken away by the security forces. Vast numbers of people are in jail, and almost a quarter—can you imagine a quarter of the five million people in my country?—are now refugees. Many of them are displaced inside the country, the others outside.

What this means for the majority of Salvadorans is suffering. It is very hard, very painful. But in El Salvador, as in Guatemala, Nicaragua, and Honduras, as in all Central America, the suffering—and this is also very biblical—gives us great strength. We feel very united as a people. We feel very strong, and we are completely sure that someday we will build new societies in Central America based on peace and justice. In preparation for that dawn of justice, we are working very, very hard for our promised land, which someone has said will be a promised land of beans and tortillas.

Under the present injustice and oppression, however, many Central Americans have no choice but to come to the United States. As you know, the United States is playing an important role in relation to the struggle and the wars in Central America. I believe that this is a great, a beautiful opportunity for the American people to work with us to build a community, to be together. The American people have this opportunity because from every Salvadoran and Guatemalan refugee you can hear a history of what our people are experiencing and suffering in our homelands. This is an opportunity for all of us to unite in solidarity. As a Salvadoran, I want to thank the many North Americans for the risks they are taking and for all they are doing to give sanctuary to the hundreds of Central Americans that come. To all of you who have been faithful to the call of God, we say sincerely: "We want to be your neighbors, we want to be your friends in Central America."

A Guatemalan Soldier Changes Sides—Rodrigo

I am a Guatemalan and I was a member of the army of the Guatemalan government for a long time. People should not be shocked by the red bandana I must wear over my face in public, even though I myself am afraid of it. I feel horrible wearing the bandana. To me it feels like a bloody bandana, like many of the handkerchiefs our people have had to use to take care of their wounds. It reminds me of the many times we were invited to be part of the death squads.

I remember how they were teaching us to torture; tortures that are very, very difficult to imagine. I remember clearly the blood that has been spilled by our people, even though I never murdered or tortured anyone. This is a very small part of the whole program of repression of the United States against our people. I remember how it was in the particular case of Guatemala. We have seen the military who came from the north with all kinds of campaigns to repress and hurt our people. We will never be able to forget how we saw them come or how they have been able to involve all their allies in this military strategy. As if their own presence were not enough, they have brought military advisers from Taiwan, Chile, and Israel. In the last few weeks we have learned that South Africa is also starting a relationship with Guatemala for the purpose of supporting the military strategy.

I believe that the sanctuary movement transcends anything we are able to imagine right now. I don't know if many of us have reflected on the anguish and the fear that the heroes and martyrs of our people were facing when they were ready to die. I have visited many communities where they have sanctuary in various parts of the United States. And I have found that there is a common question: "How can we stop the militarization of power and the military strategy of Central America, in particular in Guatemala?" And I have been able to sift through that question and see that many times we have forgotten the blood that has been spilled by our people. Those dead are not only our dead, they are also your dead.

Many people have problems understanding that we cannot build a nation with the principle of equality without first destroying the military strategy and the military power that dominates that region of the continent. It is not enough to change presidents. We are not even able to change the party in power or the generals in power who are the representatives of all the military. What we need is to change the structure of our society. Only in that way will we be able to build the new society, that kingdom that will have justice and equality as its basis. I have also seen in my visits throughout the United States that many people are trying to study, read, and inform themselves. And that is very good if it does not become the sole priority and only an intellectual exercise.

Getting information is not enough to create the new world with justice that we must bring about. And we don't need to say that we are Christians, or go to church or be related to the church, as long as we are committed to the mandate of God. We still have a lot to learn. But I continue to think of all those dead that I cannot erase from my mind. We Guatemalans want to remind you that sanctuary, as a symbol of the people of the United States' solidarity with us, becomes a very beautiful sign of hope. Someday, tomorrow, we will be able to ensure that all the blood that has been spilled has not been spilled in vain and begin to build the very beautiful future that is waiting for the people of Central America. Let sanctuary be a homage to all that blood that has been spilled. Each one of us has a responsibility in this very difficult and harsh reality that we are living now to pay homage to those victims we must keep in our minds and in our hearts.

I would like to challenge all those people who are members of the armed forces and security and intelligence forces of the government of Guatemala: they do not have to allow themselves to be used as instruments of repression. I call on them to desert so that there will be nobody to cooperate with the policies of intervention of the United States in Central America. In Guatemala, any young man from eighteen to thirty-five years of age is obliged to do military service. This is a law. But the people do not want to go. Why is it that they do not want to go? And why is it that even though this is a law, the law of the land, the army must force the people to join? Because the people of Guatemala (the same as in El Salvador) know what it means.

To start with, it's a discriminatory law, because the government does not really abide by it. It is really the poor who are forced to join. But the poor are not the only Guatemalans. The middle class and the rich are also Guatemalans. In the Guatemalan army, there are no middle-class soldiers, nor will you ever find the son of a rich landlord fighting in the mountains. There are also other important reasons why we do not want to join the army. One is that a soldier is forced to lose his own identity. People who do not know their roots do not know who they are, and in consequence they will be unable to understand the historical role they are meant to play at this moment. That is why the officers have been taught techniques to dehumanize the soldiers. They learned those techniques at the U.S. Army base in Panama, techniques that involve brainwashing, psychological pressure, and harsh physical stress. They are almost impossible to resist. Using brutal, racist, aggressive tactics, they destroy a person's self-image, turning him into an instrument incapable of understanding critically his own realities.

There are other elements to consider, however. There is the heroic resistance of the Guatemalan people. (I do not mean to exclude Salvadorans and other struggling Latin Americans.) And the resistance is heroic when one considers how the entire people is treated. The first thing the soldiers do when they enter a village is to denigrate the culture. They tell the people to take off their native clothes and dress like "people." They tell them to cut their ugly hair and to start talking the "right" language (namely, Spanish). It is a long and complex process.

We must also understand that, in spite of all these pressures, many soldiers retain goodwill for the people. But they are scared to express it because of all the physical and psychological pressures they have undergone. Only a minority of the soldiers have the inner strength to withstand those pressures. Some are capable of holding their brothers in captivity, of torturing them, even of murdering them. Racism exerts a very complex and deep influence. And when a person who is discriminated against and is attacked psychologbutly finds himself in a position to hurt others, it is natural for him in turn to discriminate, and in that way, he becomes brutal.

In conclusion, I think it important to point out the relationship I see between the way Native Americans here in the United States have been, and are, treated and the way we are treated. In both cases, the ultimate reason is that you must destroy a people's identity in order to retain control. Once people find their roots and their cultural identity, you cannot stop them with artillery or with tanks, still less with CIA agents and political maneuvers.

I Discovered We Are All People—Mario

I want to give you an idea about what we refugees think. To do this I will speak about two things. One is my experience in meeting people in the United States; the other, the experience I had in my own country, which was not a very lovely one. When I came to the United States, I was in sanctuary in Tucson. I met many people, but we didn't really know each other. It was only after about a year that I started to realize that we seemed to have something in common, even though I had no idea what I could have in common with the people of a foreign country. I could only see myself as a Salvadoran refugee in this country.

I am sure that many people for whom the United States is home would have a hard time trying to understand what I felt in my heart. But with time I discovered something very wonderful; I discovered that we were all people, that nationality could become secondary to the reality that all of us are people, and that the difference in the color of our skins could become even less important. With that understanding, I became really one with the North American people who had befriended me.

Now what did that mean? It meant literally becoming human again, because in El Salvador we had lost the meaning, the essence of the meaning of the word *people*, because we were not treated as people. I think of the child that I saw one day split open by a bullet. I just continued to stand with the child. Why do these people—I refer to the Salvadoran army—treat us like this? Why have they killed this child?

I was witness to a massacre in the northern province of Santa Ana in 1980. Forty people, mostly women and children, were killed, machine-gunned to death. I should have been one of them. I escaped miraculously, and I came here to this country seeking refuge, fleeing the horror of seeing that massacre of human beings. Seeing a child being destroyed, seeing a child even go without milk, that is repression. We know people can torture. In El Salvador the people in jail are often tortured by starvation. When people in power use starvation as a tool of social control, it is a social sin, as Archbishop Romero said.

How can I express what it has meant for us to see people in the United States show concern for us, take risks for us? Yet there are many, more every day, who are ready to face persecution to help us, who have learned to side with the poor, knowing that this means they are going to have to face repression, to risk being indicted and imprisoned. I know deep down that there must be something very strong in the midst of all this, in the midst of each one of us; and that is God, the faith we all share. Archbishop Romero said he did not believe in death without resurrection. Those were prophetic words. I, too, don't believe in death without a future, without a resurrection. That is why we don't have to be fearful of death today.

Why I Am in Public Sanctuary—Rosa María

As a university student, I was a volunteer worker in refugee camps under the auspices of the Catholic church, so I speak from personal experience and observation about the reasons for the massive displacement of peasants and workers in El Salvador. People become refugees primarily because of the military sweeps and the death squads. Simply to be a student was to be a suspect. Today, there are additional reasons to flee, especially the indiscriminate bombing in the countryside. The churches that responded at that time, opening their basements generously to the refugees, are clear evidence of the persecution that the refugees suffered in their native land. That response from the Catholic church, and other churches in El Salvador, I am now seeing on a larger scale here in the United States in the sanctuary movement.

The fact that I was a university student and also a volunteer worker who put together medicine kits, worked with the refugees, and collaborated in the church's efforts in the refugee camp led to my being identified as a subversive element. The humanitarian response in the United States made it possible for me to flee as a refugee, as other Salvadorans and Guatemalans have fled. It was this response of the churches to the conditions in El Salvador that led me to accept sanctuary. Thier extension of help to us opened the road to acceptance.

The reasons for our not returning to our land are fairly well known to you: the violence, the massacres, the deaths that are occurring there prohibit our return at this time. The answer to these wrongs has not been given to us by the United States government. Its refusal to grant us refugee status has only been circumvented by the sanctuary movement. It is this movement that has given us refugee status.

The fact that the sanctuary leaders who have supported us are being indicted and arrested, and that refugees also are being arrested, forces us to ask if we are justified in giving the public witness we are giving in the sanctuary movement. My answer is that the violence in El Salvador and in Guatemala is such that, given our lack of official recognition of refugee status in the United States, we have no alternative. We need this sanctuary against the violence that is occurring in our countries until we are able to return to them.

The objective of the mediation of the Catholic church in El Salvador—to bring about peace—is definitely one of the duties and obligations of the sanctuary movement. And this relates directly to our desire to return to our country. We want to return when peace has been restored, and the same is, of course, true of Guatemalan refugees.

A question frequently asked is why some leave Central America and others go to fight with the popular forces in the mountains. That is a matter of choice and judgment. The refugees who are here under the umbrella or the protection of sanctuary, with their living testimony, with their experience, are providing as valuable a service to their country as the guerrillas provide in their way. We are all in search of peace and justice. We believe in this as Christians and as a people, and we believe we share these goals with you. Our return in large measure may be dependent upon a decrease or elimination of the U.S. military aid that is only prolonging and worsening the conflict.

Before concluding, I want to say that U.S. observers who have returned from Honduras report that camps are being constructed. One detention camp, or concentration camp, is located in a place called La Esperanza. Isn't that ironic? *Esperanza* means hope. The people being detained or to be detained there are, some of them, deportees from the United States. The camps are also intended for Salvadorans who flee to Honduras without entry permits. They will automatically be interned in the camps, then deported from Honduras without having been entered on any rolls as actual refugees.

Response to All Refugees by Angela Berryman

I want to address the issue of the responses that Latin Americans are giving to their situation, keeping in mind that life is being threatened and annihilated by structural injustices, institutionalized violence, and war in all of Latin America, and in particular, in Central America.

What are the key issues in Latin America? One is injustice. As we all know, 2 percent of the population of El Salvador and Guatemala owns at least 60 percent of the arable land in those countries. In Guatemala, in the highlands, the average size farm for highland Indians was cut in half between 1955 and 1975. The average per capita income in El Salvador is $592, and it is less for peasants. Prices for basic items in Central America are very similar to prices here.

Another issue is violence and war: the violence of malnutrition, illiteracy, poor health care; the violence of war in which fifty thousand Salvadoran civilians have been killed during the last five years, and in which more than 20 percent of the population has been displaced. That is to say, one out of every 125 Salvadorans has been killed. In Guatemala, in 1982, the Episcopal Conference of the Catholic Church said that there were more than one million persons displaced within Guatemala and another one hundred thousand Guatemalan Indians on the border in Mexico. I recently read in the *New York Times* that, in the last four years, according to government statistics, one hundred thousand Indian children have lost one of their parents.

The air war in El Salvador has been increased tremendously this year. We have doubled the number of Bell helicopters that we are sending to El Salvador. Many, many Salvadorans, hundreds of non-combatants and peasants, have been killed by this air war. And in the media we have only silence. My husband and some other people were recently at the *Philadelphia Enquirer,* which is one of the better papers on Central America. They were telling the editorial board that the biggest issue in El Salvador in 1984 was the air war, not the election of Duarte, not anything else that was happening in El Salvador; yet no one was writing about that.

I think we have begun to just respond to what the administration puts out. If they say Duarte is a good guy, then we try to point out who Duarte really is. If they point out the economic aid that the United States is giving, we try to tell how the economic aid is being used in pacification. What we need to begin to do is take the initiative and put forth the real issues in Central America.

There are a lot of delegations going to El Salvador. The medical aid delegation talked about the air war and the burnings from white phosphorous and napalmlike substances. We have to get that information out. We have to begin to turn around what is happening in the media and gain control, because we want to tell what is really happening in El Salvador. We don't want to give our government's point of view; they want to tell what is convenient for them to tell. We need to use the materials that are available and get to the press on what the real issues are in El Salvador and Guatemala.

In Guatemala, the countryside is militarized. Thousands of Guatemalan peasants are being placed in model villages; nine hundred thousand Indian men are in civil patrols. These civil patrols and these model villages are another way of destroying the indigenous culture. What is worse is that this is not being done to protect the civilian population. They are employed and must participate in the patrols in order to protect the army.

U.S. intervention is a major issue in Central America. The United States is orchestrating an overall military, economic, political, and diplomatic strategy whose central purpose is the defeat of the insurgents in El Salvador and Guatemala—and, I would add, the defeat of the Salvadoran and Guatemalan people and, if possible, the overthrow of the Nicaraguan government. A related issue is liberation. The people of Central America do not want anything different than we want. They want the right to self-determination. As they say in Nicaragua, they are working for the logic of the majorities, that the majority of the people be served. Another issue in Central America is peace. The Central Americans, the Guatemalans, the Salvadorans, and the Nicaraguans want peace, but war has been forced on them. Let me add here that what is a nonissue in Central America is elections—contrary to what is said here in the United States. Liberation, peace, U.S. policy, violence, and injustice are the issues.

What have been some of the responses in Central America? One of the responses has been war. It is not a war that Salvadorans or Guatemalans have chosen, it is a war that has been forced on them. Another response is negotiations. We heard on 15 October 1984 a lot about the peace talks in La Palma. Since 1981, the people, in the form of the opposition movements, in the form of the churches, have been asking for negotiations. A negotiation process should be both comprehensive, that is, involve the region as a whole, yet separate in particular conflicts. The process will be different because the conflicts are different. There is no symmetry between the conflicts in El Salvador and Nicaragua. The contras on the Nicaraguan border are being trained and financed by an outside power, by the United States. In El Salvador the conflict is quite different; it is a civil war, a war of liberation. Unfortunately the conditions do not exist at this point for a mediated solution or negotiations in Guatemala.

Let me comment briefly on the Contadora process, in which Latin American nations—Mexico, Venezuela, Colombia, and Panama—have taken it upon themselves to work for peace in the region.

The leaders of the Contadora countries were united in the view that the problems of that region cannot be solved by armed force but only by political solutions springing from the region itself. They called on the Central American states to continue to make every effort to bring the Contadora process rapidly to final fruition through the signing of a comprehensive agreement that would bring peace to the region. This was a joint communique at the meeting in San José, Costa Rica, in 1984 attended by foreign ministers of the European Economic Community, the Central American countries, and the Contadora countries. What is impeding the advancement of the Contadora process is not the Central American countries; it is the United States.

In my brief reflections here, I have not mentioned explicitly the faith response of Central Americans. I think anybody who has had the privilege of living and working in Central America, or with the Central American refugees, fully understands that their faith is an integral part of what people are and do in Central America. It is just part of them. People see themselves as co-creators with God and liberators of themselves and their people.

I will end by quoting from Monsignor Romero: "Either we believe in a God of life or we serve the idols of death." The Central Americans, I believe, have chosen the God of life. The question for us is, Are we going to choose the God of life, or are we going to serve the idols of death?

CHAPTER 17

REFLECTIONS ON BEING A MINISTER AND REFUGEE

Marta Benavides

Because I'm a minister, a pastor, it is my duty to speak with you to bring news. All I need is to relate to you the life that I have lived with my people, the hope and the faith that we have for a new land and a solution to our problems and to have, in the back of our mind, the message, the gospel of God. Even though I am going to be as brief as possible, remember that I am a pastor, so I will reflect on Scripture also.

For the longest time, most of us in Latin America have felt that most North Americans have been fenced away from us, and now we are in the process of breaking those barriers. And I dare say that most of us who are here from our lands amongst you are not here to make friends but to tell you the truth. We have been so busy waging peace through waging war in El Salvador that there is not very much time to make friends. But there is time to make *compañeros* and *compañeras*, and that is the reason I am here. I think that is a very important reflection to make, because often we ascribe bad meanings to words, and the words *compañero* and *compañera* need to be understood. They have the same roots as *company* and *accompaniment*.

It was really because God wanted to be in our company that God in the Christian tradition sent Jesus to be with us. But those of us who believe that we are children of God have to know that we are in the company of God because we are supposed to be in God's image, and God describes himself or herself as I, the "I Am" in the Exodus. The I Am is the real life, but it is not the past and it is not the future, it is now. It is very important that we see that God is in our company because God created us. But we are in God's image. We are alike. So we are *compañeros* with God and God's creation. It is important to be *compañeros* with you.

I would like to reflect on the prospects for peace in El Salvador and in Central America. We are seriously concerned in Central America. We have come to see life destroyed so much that we are in the process of constructing life, and we use that word, *construction*. We construct life, little by little, just as a builder does, brick by brick. People have to put one brick after the other to build a big house. And it is very important that we realize that we have to build, that we have to have this revolutionary process, to go little by little creating things that endure. If we do it the easy way, we do it with no foundation.

But if we want things to last, we must build patiently. For those of us who see ourselves as children of God it's very important not only to have the revolutionary process, which means to study also, but to figure out how to have enough love, because only when we love can we denounce and announce. We cannot be the kind of people who only go around complaining and whining. We must look at the bad so we can do good. It is very, very important in this work that we live for others. Monsignor Romero wanted that very much.

It is very important that we have prospects for peace. Peace is not something that is a given; peace is something that you must fight for, that you must build, so you must have a program, you must have a method to achieve it. You have to do it in a real world. So we cannot go into a corner and brood about God sending peace, because we ourselves are to be the peacemakers.

We are supposed to be here in this world to act to change it and to transform it. And God, the I Am, has called us to get away from slavery; as we live every day, we must struggle to free ourselves. We are going to the promised land. Do you agree that we have not reached it yet? We know for sure in El Salvador that we have not reached the promised land; even after we get the beans and tortillas, we still will know that we haven't got to the promised land, because we must make sure that we get to the milk and honey, a better quality of life for each person, a society of greater equality.

Once you get the milk and honey you have to be very, very rich and creative in your imagination. One must realize that God does not want the dances and the readings and all those worshiping experiences, but demands of us, as a real, living worship, to let the rivers of justice flow. Let justice flow like rivers. Did you ever think about rivers? They start with many little creeks that finally get together in unity to become a river. But we will not create a river if we say that so and so is no good because he does not think like me, or that one is not good enough. If we believe that we have found some of the light, it is our duty to figure out how to bring others along. But part of revolutionary patience is also to remember that none of us is perfect here on this earth. So we must do the best with what we have, knowing that we are going to the promised land, knowing that we have to keep moving to get there. At times, though, we just keep looking for ways to obstruct that process. I am trying to bring to you the power that we have, because many of you probably feel sorry for us in El Salvador and Central America. We are not feeling sorry for ourselves. We can only feel sorry for ourselves if we are not up to the last moment confronting the Pharaoh. That is the only problem that we might have in El Salvador, if we are not ready to face up, to struggle.

Right now people are celebrating life in many ways. We constantly grab life away from death in El Salvador. In March of 1980, when the new junta that your government supported came into power, they declared an agrarian reform to benefit the people. That is when they also went into the rural areas and militarized everything, and that is when large numbers of rural poor people started to go through the mountains by every possible back way to hide in the city. The peasants came, and they asked Monsignor for help. And Monsignor said: "Marta, help them." Monsignor believed in unity and ecumenity. And I said to Mons—that's what I called him—"But Mons, what are we going to do?" He replied: "Think about it, daughter, you'll find out what to do." And I said, "Oh, how about the other Christians who speak English and other languages? We will call them, we need help urgently." And your community started to respond. But we ourselves had to respond right then and there.

And the government said: "We are doing very good things here in El Salvador for the people; we are an agrarian country and we need to solve this inequality." But part of what they were doing by enforcing agrarian reform was to find those people who were leaders and who believed in equality and kill them. That's what they were doing. And when the people ran away from those areas and came to us for help and we responded, the government said: "If they run away, that is proof enough that they are subversives, and those who help them are as subversive as they are."

We had to set up the refugee centers. We had to set up all the things to respond to the people. But at the same time we also called other churches and other humanitarian institutions in the world to come and see what was going on there. Some people said, "That's very political." So it is. But aren't we supposed to do whatever is necessary to defend life? We should not be afraid to know that we are political. Each one of us is political. And it is very important that we know that even when we choose to be neutral, we are being political. But, it is very political also when I go to Corpus Christi and the leader, the boss of the newspaper there, tells the reporters: "You cannot go to the press conference with that person because whoever is promoting that here has ulterior motives." Well, whoever stopped the press conference also had ulterior motives, and a lot of times we don't see that. We must become of a critical mind and be willing to take the stance that we have to confront and be strong. Also, we should not be afraid to be called names.

The first place I was called a communist was in the United States of America. When I was studying at the seminary, I tried very hard to do good work with a youth group in a church. But I told my superiors that I had to work with people who would help me to figure out how to continue working with my people in El Salvador, because I had come to learn, the good and the bad. So I decided eventually that I would not go and work at the church with the youth group. I had to go and work with the farm workers so they could teach me, because they were the people most similar to my people.

At the seminary they said: "But who is going to supervise you?" And I said: "The people are, and my conscience is." "Oh, no," they said, "who's going to give you grades?" "God," I told them. They didn't believe that. But we fought, and I won. And the people taught me that what they needed was not little tracts or Bibles in Spanish, but for me to understand that they were suffering, that the Puerto Ricans and the Chicanos were suffering from exile. Even though they lived in Texas, the Chicanos did not want to relocate to New Jersey.

And even though the Puerto Ricans are American citizens (they were declared American citizens by force in 1917, right at the time of the war, so they could be drafted), they didn't want to be in the United States; but if they were not here, they could not feed their families. I kept scratching my head, saying, "How do I minister to migrant farm workers?" The only way was to develop a movement with them and together find a way. We worked very hard and did not sleep at night trying to figure out the next day, and the next, and the next.

We formed an organization to defend the rights of the people and challenge the employers who were not paying Social Security, and the county that received money for health services for the farm workers, providing jobs for doctors, nurses, and teachers' aides, while the farm workers could not get the services. I would go and have big fights with the doctor, and he would say, "Cutie, don't be worried about these things. You are a nice little kid, get out of this kind of work."

And then I said, "Enough! I had better take a bunch of farm workes along that can defend themselves, and beat up the doctor if needed." Then the people in the church started to say: "It used to be nice to talk with Marta when she was Christian, but now she is a communist." Then some of the church people rejected me because they said I was a communist.

At that time I didn't know what communism was, so I went to the county Library, and I asked the librarian, because you are supposed to deal with things—"check them out," as they say. So, I went to check it out, and the librarian said, "What are you talking about? Communist books?"

"Yes," I said. She said, "You have to go to Philadelphia to get those books," and she frowned at me. But I tell you, I went. I went to look for the books, and some of the books were very hard to read, especially since I did not know English well. But still I had to check it out, and I found out that some of the concepts were common sense and I should not be worried. I did not meet any communists in South Jersey, but we still had to fight very hard with the farmers, because they decided that we were communists and they were going to kick us out of there. However, the issue is not people who out of ignorance and insecurity do things like that. The issue is when we know it and we allow it, when we submit ourselves to this.

Why am I speaking about these things in terms of prospects for peace? Because I am trying to insist that it requires hard work in order to be at peace. Peace is at hand, peace is available, but we have to grab it. In the Bible it also says that the Kingdom of God suffers violence and only those who dare can work for peace. It means that we have to live a very daring life. It means that we should know what Contadora is and we should know that the United States is trying to destroy Contadora. It means that we should be able to be informed enough to know that when they have the peace talks in El Salvador, we have to support that. But we should also know that the peace talks were held in order to take away from the visibility of Contadora and to prevent the Contadora treaty from being signed. It means that we must not allow conflict in Central America to be seen in terms of East vs. West, but rather as the result of inequality and exploitation. We think being a pacifist means not fighting. Being a pacifist really means making peace, and making peace requires work.

As I conclude, I want to stress again that I am an exile myself. So I speak as one. For the work that I did with Monsignor Romero, the government of El Salvador, with the support of the U.S. government, charged me, and they went to capture me at my house. There are all kinds of stories in El Salvador about how I jumped over roofs and so on, but that is not true. I was in the church working when somebody came to warn me. And an international worker gave me "sanctuary" that day in his jeep and took me out of the church. And then, from there on, I had to continue working underground. I had to because it was my decision to do it. Many of us who are exiles feel like permanent autumn, like a leaf that is forever just going with the wind from here to there.

But we know that there will be roots and that we are going to plant our corn again. But to do it, we need the support of our U.S. *compañeros*! Sanctuary is not just a project. The people have to be our sanctuary, have to feel with us. What does "solidarity" mean? Solidarity is not liquid—liquid stuff you can stick your hand in. Solidarity means to be solid; you are so solid with us, we are one.

We must know that our solidarity will make Central America a sanctuary for its people. But solidarity means working with the East-West problem and a lot of inequality in your very own country, such as with the Native Americans, the blacks, and women. That is very much a part of the oppression and repression that exists in Central America. We the people in El Salvador, and Latin America—and I know because I know Latin America very well—believe in development. But we believe that there cannot be development for our peoples without having a better quality of life, and this quality of life is an absence of war. But it is not only the military war from which we are suffering, it is also the miserable existence of our people. That is the reason we have to wage war to wage peace.

And so, at this point, whatever we are doing has to do with stopping the war. As we are trying to stop the war we must do it in a way that is also preparing to defend and to reconstruct. Everything we are doing has those qualities: stopping the war and figuring out through this process of stopping the war how to start building, how to develop the kinds of skills and knowledge and commitment that are going to allow us to defend and to rebuild the nation.

We are already rebuilding, and those who are doing sanctuary work properly here are already rebuilding. It is also important to give the kind of support to the refugees that enables them to learn skills also. They need to be challenged and also supported in their commitment to go back home. Some are already going back home; many of my friends have gone back to start this process, even though some of us are exiles. Even those who have accepted sanctuary have not accepted to stay away. We Salvadorans have to find the solution, which has to be stopping the war and working for defense and reconstruction right now. And the same challenge faces the people of the United States. They must do the same thing for the people of El Salvador, for the people of Nicaragua, for the people of Guatemala, and for their very own selves.

CHAPTER 18

WAGING PEACE
Jim Wallis

A Norwegian pastor, so the story goes, was called in to Gestapo headquarters during World War II. Before the conversation began, the Gestapo officer pulled his Luger out of its holster and laid it on the desk between himself and the pastor. Almost instinctively the pastor reached into his satchel, pulled out his Bible, and placed it on the desk beside the Luger. "Why did you do that?" the Gestapo officer asked. The pastor replied, "You have put your weapon on the table, and so have I."

Like this Norwegian pastor, people in the sanctuary movement are increasingly putting their weapon on the table by quoting the Bible in and out of court, especially now that they have been attacked by the authorities. The problem confronting the U.S. government is that too many people have been reading the Bible. To read the Bible with your eyes wide open to the world around you will always get you into trouble.

When we were in seminary years ago, we did an experiment. We took an old Bible and found every single reference to the poor in the Old and New Testaments, finding several thousand verses on the subject. It was an exhaustive study by young, zealous, evangelical seminarians.

When we finished the study, one of our number wanted to see what would happen if he took a pair of scissors to that old Bible and cut out of it every reference to the poor. And so he did. It took him a very, very long time.

When he was finished, we were left with a Bible that was literally falling apart and coming unglued; it was a Bible that was full of holes. And I used to take that Bible out with me to preach and hold it high in the air and say, "Brothers and sisters, this is the American Bible full of holes from all we have taken out."

Not just our friends on the right, but all of us, have a tendency to not want the biblical word to speak to us. Instead, we want to find in the Bible justification for our assumptions and preconceptions and what we already believe. More and more I find it to be a discomforting thing to read the Bible. It seems to overturn most of our assumptions. And one of the things upon which the Bible is clear is God's defense of and God's love for those who are always on the bottom of everybody else's list of priorities.

Rather than any of us being self-righteous or judging those on the right or the left, we had better open our Bibles together and try to let that word speak to us and teach us all some new and different lessons.

Here are some particularly useful paragraphs from Matthew 25, together with an up-to-date paraphrase: "For I was hungry and you gave me food, I was thirsty and you gave me drink, I was a stranger and you welcomed me, I was naked and you clothed me, I was sick and you visited me, I was in prison and you came to me."

"I was a refugee. I had to flee my country, my father and brother were killed, my mother and sister were raped. They took my husband, and he was tortured, and now he is dead. I knew they would come for me. I was afraid for my child, so I fled and came to a strange country.

"I was alone, I had no one, you took me in. You welcomed me into your church and into your family. You opened your doors for me; you opened your heart for me."

"And all the people were astonished," the Bible says, and they said, in effect: "Lord, we didn't know it was you. When did we see you hungry? When did we see you thirsty? When did we see you naked, a stranger, sick, and in prison? When did we see you a refugee?"

"Truly, truly I say to you, as you did it to one of the least of these, you did it to me."

What is at stake here? Far more than a political issue, far more than all the legal questions that we are now embroiled in, far more than questions of public policy. More than all of that. What is at stake is what we can see and whose face we see in the faces of those who come to us as strangers and sojourners.

Every Saturday morning in our neighborhood there is a food line. At 6:00 A.M. people come and get in line, and it is 8:30 before the door opens. But every Saturday morning when we all begin, we join hands and say a prayer, and Mrs. Glover normally prays. She is an elderly black woman, and she prays like someone who knows to whom she is speaking. Every time, her prayer is something like this: "Lord, we know that you will be coming through the line today. So Lord, help us to treat you well. Help us to treat you well."

The sanctuary movement that began with compassion has come to confrontation. Compassion has become illegal. The U.S. government is on a collision course with the religious community and with millions of U.S. citizens across this country over its policies in Central America. In January 1985, just before the opening of a major conference on sanctuary in Tucson, Arizona, the government moved massively against the sanctuary movement by arresting refugees and indicting clergy and laity who harbor and transport them, who follow the biblical mandate to provide hospitality, the holy hospitality of God.

A few days later, there was more evidence of that confrontation. In a meeting at the U.S. Department of State, a delegation announced to this government that 42,352 of its citizens had signed a Pledge of Resistance; half of these are prepared to go to jail if the United States escalates its military aggression in Central America.

Looking at the document that gives a state-by-state breakdown of how many people have signed this Pledge of Resistance, one sees something very impressive. A letter delivered to Secretary of State George Schultz said this:

More than 40,000 U.S. citizens are sending a clear signal to their government by making a simple but serious pledge—a Pledge of Resistance. On the basis of our most deeply held religious and moral convictions, we are unalterably opposed to present U.S. policies in Central America. . . . It is always appropriate and responsible for the religious community and others of good will to seek to prevent senseless violence and the suffering it causes. . . .

To break the law is a serious thing for us, but we have seen the U.S. government violate international law and moral conscience every day in Central America. To halt that illegality and immorality, tens of thousands of U.S. citizens are ready to resist our government's war against the people of Central America to the point of going to jail, if necessary.

Craig Johnstone, deputy assistant secretary of state for inter-American affairs, was told: "There is now a new factor you must consider. The domestic cost of your military escalation will be to imprison tens of thousands of your own citizens." And I want to report to you that Mr. Johnstone was sobered by that promise.

I believe that the arrests were timed with both the Tucson conference and the Pledge of Resistance—which is growing around the country—in mind. They were designed to take the focus off the moral questions and put it on merely legal questions, to take the government off trial, to keep it from having to defend U.S. policy in Central America, and to force us to defend ourselves.

However, the policy is not working. For centuries people have sought what has been called the moral equivalent of war—namely, waging peace. Risk taking has always been a part of war—soldiers leave home and jobs and families and security to go to faraway places and risk their lives—but more and more Americans are beginning to discover that risks must also be taken for peace.

We have begun to talk about what it means to wage peace, with the same discipline and sacrifice and willingness to suffer with which so many people have waged war. Waging peace has increasingly come to mean moving beyond protest, adopting different forms of protest, inventing new ways to resist.

The sanctuary movement, Witness for Peace, the Pledge of Resistance, the free South Africa movement, and so many other examples spreading across the country indicate that discernible decision, that step from protest to resistance. Protest is speaking; resistance is acting. To protest is to say that something is wrong; to resist is to try to stop it. To protest is to raise your voice; to resist is to stand up and put your body on the line. To protest is to say you disagree; to resist is simply to flatly say no. To move from protest to resistance is indeed a serious step, but more and more of us believe that our present situation is so serious that such a step is called for.

Those of us who are Christians remember the words of Jesus: "Blessed are the peacemakers, for they shall be called children of God." But perhaps we have misunderstood the words for many years. It's almost as if we have heard Jesus saying: "Blessed are the peace lovers." But he doesn't say that.

It is not those who only love peace who will be called the children of God. It is those who make peace. And making peace always leads to confrontation, as is so evident in the life of Jesus and every other peacemaker. Blessed are the peacemakers, for they shall be called the children of God.

It is indeed very possible that such strong actions, taking risks and making sacrifices, may indeed stir conscience in this land, change minds, soften hearts, and awaken the public. We have seen that happen before. But I would suggest that there are issues at stake deeper than political effectiveness. There are issues of personal faith and personal responsibility.

We do not know if we can win, but we do know what the gospel says. We do not know if the military madness can be stopped, but we do know that God calls us to be peacemakers. We do not know if invasions and interventions can be halted, but we do know that God cares about the victims and that we must stand in the way of our government's violence against them.

As North Americans we come out of a tradition that makes us accustomed to winning. We think that if we really do something serious—like declaring sanctuary or signing a Pledge of Resistance—certainly after a while what we have done will produce the desired result. But the people of Central America are teaching all of us that we must have a much longer-range perspective. These people, who have given and committed and resisted and suffered so much more than any of us, and who maintain hope in the midst of all that, and who continue and continue without—in most cases—tangible or visible success, have much to teach us. Their long-term perspective is what we have to develop. On political grounds alone, we are not going to see short-term success in these movements. The resources of faith we have to bring to bear are very important.

Our actions are new factors in U.S. government decision making. A short time ago two hundred top military personnel met at the National War College. The speaker was a high-ranking general. He told his audience that the greatest challenge to them today comes from the churches. The military, he said, must take into account the whole new way of thinking that is developing in the churches. This shows the significance of the beginning efforts of which we constitute a humble part.

We also have to remember that we are part of a long tradition of people who didn't see immediate results from their commitments and efforts and yet maintained hope. And we are standing on the shoulders of those women and men who have gone before us. It is not going to be an easy struggle or one that gives quick results, which just means that we have to go deeper than we have gone before into our own faith and resolve.

We do not know when the poor will see justice, but we do know that our God stands among the poor and invites us to join him there. The time has come for us to take personal responsibility. And that becomes an even deeper reason for acting, deeper even than the hope of success.

We must always remember that history has been changed when individuals and small groups of people began to take personal responsibility, usually for reasons of faith or conscience, and thereby opened up new possibilities in their lives and in the lives of others. Breakthroughs are possible, but only through a deeper level of commitment. Our prayer of resistance is a prayer for the grace of God to enable us to make that deeper commitment.

The powers that be are counting on our losing hope. It could be said that that is *their* hope. Some people in high places are just waiting for us to wear down or wear out. But it is the persistence of our hope, even in the midst of their seeming domination, that is the single greatest threat to their absolute authority.

David MacMichael, who used to work in the CIA, said in a *Sojourners* interview, "True power consists of being able to require others to accept your reality."[1] He also said that we can't imagine the anger within the CIA and the top echelons of power directed toward those people who refuse to accept official definitions of reality but hold up an alternative view. They are furious about people in opposition movements, because every voice, however small, however marginal, however ineffectual, challenges their monopoly on defining reality.

I believe we have to come to terms more deeply than we have with what we are confronting more and more in this country—lawless authority. Lawless authority defines itself as legal and those who disobey as illegal. It is in our best traditions, religious and moral, to resist lawless authority in the name of conscience and law, but in so doing, we will be deemed illegal, and we will be put in jail. Authority has become more and more lawless, not only on sanctuary, but also on nuclear weapons, on all of U.S. policy. And to love conscience and law is to resist lawless authority. For that, we are going to be found disobedient, and we are going to pay the price of those who break the law. We have to come to terms with that politically, morally, emotionally, and spiritually.

To hope against the power of the authorities is to undermine the illusions and control they depend upon. But the poor of the world are hoping we don't give up, for it is their lives at stake. Our despair and resignation will do them no good at all. In fact, only in hope can we join with the poor in the quest for justice and freedom. For the poor and for those who struggle at their side, hope is not a feeling or a mood, but a necessity for survival. It is important to remember that hope means more than just hanging on. Hope is the conscious decision to see the world in a different way. Hope is to look through the eyes of faith to a future not determined by oppressive circumstances that we now can see. Hope is to know that the present reality will not have the last word, that despite the pretensions and the cruelties of idolatrous authorities, God rules. And God will have the last word.

There is a story about how a verse was added to that great freedom hymn "We Shall Overcome." The song itself is said to be an old hymn that goes way back in the black church. Later it became a labor song and finally the great civil rights anthem that we all know so well. The lyrics were put together at the Highlander Center in the hills of Tennessee. The story goes that one weekend at the Highlander Center, a black youth choir had come in for a retreat. They were in the chapel on their last night, singing and just enjoying being together. They had sung "We Shall Overcome" earlier in the evening.

But near the end of the evening, the chapel was surrounded by members of the local White Citizens Council. They came brandishing shotguns and carrying torches, and they ordered the young people out of the chapel into the darkness. But the kids wouldn't budge. The intruders became more insistent, demanding they come outside, so the lights in the chapel were turned off.

The air was filled with tension and fear, but all of a sudden in a corner of the chapel a single voice began to sing. The tune was familiar, but the words were new. The words were these: "We are not afraid, we are not afraid, we shall overcome someday." The voices of the White Citizens Council were drowned out, and they left that night in frustration. A new verse to an old song had just been written.

Those young people of another era were not afraid, because they knew something. Today members of the sanctuary movement are being arraigned in court for one reason, a reason that has nothing to do with immigration law or national security. They are being arraigned because the government hopes that they will be afraid— and that we will be afraid. But together we will say, in the words of that great old song, "We are not afraid, we are not afraid, we shall overcome someday."

NOTES

1. David MacMichael, *Sojourners*, August 1984, p. 22.

CHAPTER 19

THE TASKS AHEAD
William Sloane Coffin

We in the sanctuary movement say "Bless you" to those indicted and arrested. We answer to the many Guatemalans, Salvadorans, and other Central Americans here in this country and still there in Central America who are pleading with us to help them stop the carnage. And we wish to remind the Immigration and Naturalization Service (INS) of Thoreau's words: "They are lovers of the law who uphold it when the government breaks it."

We in the sanctuary movement make no apology for what we are doing. It is an evil thing forcibly to deport innocent civilians to possible detention, torture, and death. Were the U.S. government today forcibly returning Soviet Jews to the Soviet Union, or Poles to Poland, neither the Congress nor the American people would stand for it.

Why then do so many sit idly by when innocent Salvadorans are being returned to a country whose death squads long ago would have killed Lech Walesa? Why do they tolerate the forceful repatriation of Guatemalans to a government widely viewed as the most brutal in the entire Western hemisphere?

In 1980, Congress passed a refugee act that recognized political asylum as the right due those fleeing persecution. It is a good law. But it is being miserably misinterpreted by the INS. While correctly classifying as political refugees people escaping a variety of communist lands, the INS insists on labeling Salvadorans and Guatemalans as economic refugees and, as such, deportable. The reason is transparent. To call "political" refugees from countries whose governments our own enthusiastically supports with military and economic aid would raise all kinds of embarrassing questions.

Because it has knowingly deported innocent people to torture and death, the Reagan administration has blood on its hands. And if it has, it is because the Congress and the American people have water on theirs, water like Pilate's. Now nuns, priests, ministers, and Christian laity are being indicted for doing God's holy work of hospitality. The arrest of church leaders will only strengthen the sanctuary movement, whose true leader lies just beyond the reach of the INS. But what do such arrests, if they continue, and the continued deportation of innocent Guatemalans and Salvadorans, say about the callousness of the Congress, about the willingness of the American people to tolerate activity so blatantly un-American?

Congress could put the sanctuary movement out of business tomorrow by doing one of two things: Insist that the Refugee Act of 1980 be properly administered according to both the spirit and the letter of the law, or alternatively, pass a so-called extended voluntary departure act, which would allow Salvadorans and Guatemalans to remain in this country until such time as it was deemed safe for them to return home.

We in the sanctuary movement should do everything in our power—phone calls, individual letters, letters from church and synagogue bodies, to persuade Congress to follow one of these two paths. Were Congress to do so, the sanctuary task of the sanctuary movement would be accomplished; however, much would remain to be done. For we have pledged ourselves to attenuate suffering, not only here in the States, but also there in Central America. We simply have to change U.S. policy there.

According to the view of the Reagan administration, the current revolt in El Salvador is inspired and sustained from abroad. But as Carlos Fuentes testified two years ago, if Cuba and Nicaragua were to sink beneath the sea and the Soviet Union contract to the size of medieval Novgorod, the local bitter conflict in El Salvador would continue. It is born and bred in local oppression.

Let's face it, not even revolutionaries make revolutions. Revolutions are manufactured by repressive governments that grind the poor into the dust. President Kennedy was right: "Those who make peaceful evolution impossible make violent revolution inevitable."

What we the American people must realize is finally quite simple: You cannot have a revolt without revolting conditions. The fire can't spread unless the wood is dry. It is when the oligarchs are few—when 10 percent of Guatemalan citizens prosper on 82 percent of the land—that the guerrillas become many.

Of course there are Marxists in Central America, lots of them. Capitalism has not been kind to the people of those countries. But all Marxists in this world are not Stalinists. As a matter of fact, Stalinism is to Marxism what the Ku Klux Klan is to Christianity, a manipulation of the symbols in order to deny the reality. Furthermore, as a former (non-Marxist) president of Venezuela wrote, "Latin American revolutionaries are attracted to the promises of Marxism, not to Soviet power." When are we Americans going to realize that the Soviet Union is so bankrupt—morally, intellectually, economically—that it is today the only country in the world surrounded by hostile communist countries?

What is so sad in all this is that so many North Americans have forgotten so much of their recent history. It was sixty-three years ago that Charles Evans Hughes announced that we are seeking to establish a "pax Americana." He was secretary of state, serving President Coolidge, who—as he dispatched the Marines into Nicaragua for the fourteenth time in Nicaraguan history—explained, "We are saving Nicaragua from the Bolsheviks."

Ten years later, in 1933, Cordell Hull proclaimed Roosevelt's Good Neighbor Policy, which signaled a shift from unilateral action to collective action and resulted fifteen years later (in 1948) in the formation of the Organization of American States. But alas, just over the horizon was the cold war, bringing with it a fresh onslaught of blind anticommunism. In 1954, the CIA overthrew the duly elected government of Arbenz in Guatemala. In 1960, the CIA sponsored an invasion of Cuba. In 1965, the Marines landed once again in the Dominican Republic. In 1973, Nixon and Kissinger tried to destabilize the Allende government of Chile, and today in Nicaragua, El Salvador, Honduras, and Guatemala, the North American Eagle is once again fastening its talons on lands not its own. In a figure of speech used by a former president of Guatemala, "The North American shark is eating Latin American sardines."

But it's not just blind anticommunism that drives us, although sometimes I think the most powerful ideology in this world in terms of unexamined slogans and premises is not communism but anticommunism. Wish fulfillment is also involved. We wish to believe the destinies of Central America are being designed in Havana and Moscow; then we are free to redesign them in Washington.

The fact is that the United States wants to continue to control what goes on south of its border, in the same way that the Soviet Union wants to control what goes on in Afghanistan. It's not a matter of security in either case; it's a matter of pride, good old-fashioned nationalistic pride.

In the fourth chapter of Luke, as many of you know, the devil takes Jesus up to a high place and shows him "all the kingdoms of the world in a moment of time." Then the devil says: "All this dominion will I give to you, and the glory that goes with it." The temptation is to seek status through power. If it was a temptation for Jesus, you can imagine what a temptation it is for a superpower—quite irresistible!

If we don't understand what is going on south of the border, it is because our pride-swollen faces have closed up our eyes. It is because our ears are stopped to the cries of those who say, in effect: "We are not taking orders any more from the U.S. ambassador."

But there is yet another reason for our misguided actions, a third reason beyond blind anticommunism and a desire for continued control. The older I get, the more I am persuaded that foreign policy to an extraordinary degree reflects a government's attitude toward its own people. For instance, were our government concerned that 50 percent of black youth in our cities are today unemployed, were our government serious in its desire to combat racism at home, it would never have come up with "constructive engagement," a policy in South Africa called by Bishop Tutu an "unmitigated disaster."

Or look at it this way: Our foreign aid today to Central America is making the rich richer, the poor poorer, and the military more powerful. Isn't that exactly what is happening in our own country? Are not the farmers who have been protesting in the freezing cold in Chicago and in Minnesota demonstrating that the need for land redistribution in this country is fast becoming as urgent as it is in El Salvador?

There have been endless revolutions and coups d'état in Central and South America. Most of them simply replace one head of state with another, leaving untouched the pyramid of power and property relationships. But occasionally when they or a duly elected government sought to turn the pyramid upside down, to end the exploitation of the many by the few, to put the needs of the many poor at the top of the national agenda—Guatemala under Arbenz, Cuba under Castro, Chile under Allende, Grenada under Maurice Bishop, Nicaragua today—the government of the United States reacted with fury. In other words, what our government seems most to fear is precisely what the millions of Latin America most long for—a successful economic and social revolution.

We always pose the issue in terms of civil liberties: freedom versus communism, freedom versus totalitarianism. But the real issue is human rights in economic and social terms. The real issue is the pyramid of property and power relationships. In other words, a successful social revolution, let us say in Nicaragua or El Salvador, would not only be a beacon of hope to enlighten the darkness of Central and South America; it would also cast a few enlightening rays in our direction. And that, I suggest, is what our government, consciously or unconsciously, fears the most.

If my analysis is correct, if only in part, we in the sanctuary movement can no longer separate foreign policy from domestic policies, and we may have to recognize that the best way to change the former lies in a change of the latter. I realize that by making these connections, the sanctuary movement may lose some of its middle-class adherents, but only by making these connections will the movement gain converts among the poor in this country, especially blacks, who tend to resent so much attention being lavished on "foreigners" when they could use a little more attention themselves.

In any case, our immediate task is clear. We must continue the sanctuary movement in its present form until Congress makes it unnecessary to do so. Beyond asking for extended voluntary departure, we must plead with the Congress immediately to stop the funding of the contras, which is in violation of law—of the Boland amendment and all kinds of laws of the UN and of the OAS. And of course Congress must slow down (not to mention stop) rather than increase military aid to El Salvador, so that the military there will have to allow Duarte to negotiate an end to the conflict. In addition, I would enthusiastically invite the Contadora nations in. Mediation is exactly what this country needs, if only we have the humility to accept it.

Because we are a religious movement, we must remain loving and hopeful. Of course we hate what is evil, but only because we so love the good. If you hate evil more than you love the good, you end up a damned good hater. And of such we have enough. We are not going to become frustrated and bitter. We know that rarely in this world does a good deed go unpunished. We know that in the upcoming important trial in Phoenix, the argument that makes that trial important will probably not be allowed in court. We know that the Congress and the American people may be slow in responding to our urgent pleas.

But never mind. Love is a long-distance runner. "Love never ends." So ours will be the hope of the psalmist: "At nightfall, weeping enters in, but with the dawn rejoicing"[1]; or that of Isaiah, who promised: "They that hope in the Lord will renew their strength, they will soar as with eagles' wings; they will run and not grow weary, walk and not grow faint."[2]

We shall not forget the reassurance of Him who told us we would in this world have tribulation, but to be of good cheer because He had overcome the world. Let us, therefore, "sing a song full of the faith that our dark past has brought us, a song full of the hope that the present has brought us. Facing the rising sun of a new day begun, let us march on til victory is won."

NOTES

1. Psalm 30:6.
2. Isaiah 40:31.

CHAPTER 20

THE COVENANT AS SANCTUARY
Jim Corbett

> Will those who are not Jews or Christians or Muslims allow us to give Abraham's name to those who are called to serve? Of course other races and religions can use an equivalent name which is more appropriate to their tradition. And you, my brothers and sisters who are atheistic humanists, don't think you have been forgotten. Translate what I say in my language into your language. When I talk of God, translate, perhaps, by "nature," "evolution," what you will. If you feel in you the desire to use the qualities you have, if you think selfishness is narrow and choking, if you hunger for truth, justice, and love, you can and should go with us.
>
> —DOM HELDER CAMARA, *The Desert Is Fertile*[1]

Latin America's covenant ecumenism is truly catholic. In contrast to the European ecumenical agenda of corporate mergers and homogenized beliefs, it is integrative rather than assimilative, delighting in the unreduced diversity of those who unite in service to the Kingdom. Yet, when we compare the Christian communities formed by the poor in Latin America with the communities now forming from the practice of sanctuary in the United States, we see distinctive ways that this multiconfessional openness is uniting us here in Anglo America. First, our joint practice is grafting the people that is the church onto the people that is Israel; we are—Christian and Jew—affirming in practice that we are formed by the same covenant. Second, unbelievers are being fully incorporated into covenant-formed base communities. Third, sanctuary is the needle's eye through which congregations composed of the beneficiaries of violence are entering into active community with the violated.

In both Latin America and Anglo America, the decision of the institutional church and of congregations to enter into protective community with the poor and persecuted involves efforts to hold the state accountable for its violations of human rights. This prophetic witness is central to the covenant task. It is also the activity that most often results in denunciations of the church for becoming "political" rather than remaining strictly "religious." In a broader sense, though, the charge that the church is abandoning its proper role has to do with its beginning to free itself from almost seventeen centuries of Constantinian captivity. As it joins the violated in the face of organized violence, it is ceasing to be the nominally apolitical pillar of the established powers.

In Latin America, the church's decision to stand with the poor and persecuted has initiated a new age of martyrs. For many of the faithful, this means a return to the catacombs. In Anglo America, declarations of sanctuary trade on the privileged position the church has acquired during the Constantinian captivity, which means that the sanctuary movement is inherently transitional. For example, the state's protesting tolerance of sanctuary during the Reagan administration's first term has now shifted to open attack and infiltration during the final term. But in Anglo America the church need not retreat to the catacombs as the price of liberation; conditions are ripe in the United States for establishing, through our practice of sanctuary, a sustainable social base for the defense of humanitarian and human rights laws. Because the U.S. government plays a major role in sponsoring gross violators of human rights in Latin America, our success in establishing this social base could also help to maintain some measure of aboveground "space" for Latin America's post-Constantinian church.

Sanctuary's juridically constructive relation to the state has been of little practical concern during the initial growth of the sanctuary network but is now of crucial importance. I will focus on it later, as a fourth way that the practice of sanctuary in the United States is opening distinctive opportunities for us to serve as multiconfessional convenant communities.

Peoples of the Covenant

The faiths that differentiate the churches from one another are often formulated in terms of belief as expressed in creed and rite. Faith as belief pertains essentially to individuals; the denominations represent associations of like-minded believers. But the denominations are also branches (even if latter-day grafts) of a people of many peoples that is formed by its covenanted task and that persists, bound to the fulfillment of its task, through the shifting perspectives of passing millennia and the kaleidoscopic cultural diversity of scattered exile. By covenanting to become a community that hallows the earth, congregations enter into this prophetic faith that is expressed by service rather than belief or ritual.

Individuals can resist war and injustice, but only a people can live *shalom* (harmonious community) into actuality. Everyone who chooses to serve must, therefore, discover a congregational place that permits personal integration into a covenant community and that also integrates the community into a historically persisting covenant people. Many of us trace the history of our congregational faith back to Sinai and voice our allegiance with the Lord's Prayer or the Shema, but Native Americans also tell of the community that is formed by the covenant to serve life, and the rabbis of the Talmud insist that the Way toward *shalom* is revealed to us in the unclaimed wilderness of Sinai because it has been and is offered to every people. It is "not the Torah of the Levites, nor the Torah of the Israelites, but the Torah of Humankind whose gates are open to receive the righteous nation which keeps the truth and those who are good and upright in their hearts."[2]

Because each person, congregation, and nation occupies a unique place in time and space, the service required is unforeseeable. Far from demanding a preconceived uniformity, the covenant requires openness to continual discovery—that is, to being addressed personally by all we meet. It requires faith as trust rather than preconception. We are addressed as a people through the course of our generations, so community study, consultation, and reflection are the context of personal and congregational response, but neither address nor response can be conjured or programmed. On the side of our being personally addressed, faithful service is alert readiness to meet "I-am-present-as-I-am-present."[3] On the side of responsive personal presence, faithful service means filling our historically unrepeatable place. ("On the day of judgment," Rabbi Zusya observes, "I will not be asked why I was not Moses but, rather, why I was not Zusya."[4]) In other words, the prophetic faith requires our personal participation as man-and-woman community-in-history "made in the image" of the unimageable source of creation; we are to co-create the human aspect of *shalom*.

A Faith for Unbelievers

Excluding a person from the exercise of co-creative initiative is the foundational form of violence, marginalizing both the violated and their violators. Genuine community, to the contrary, is a place of empowerment. Some traditions call this vitalizing incorporation communion. Gathering to seek guidance, we find that Scripture and other prophecy address us primarily as a community and call for a community response. We are to live together in ways that hallow the earth with peace and justice, and this power is not in the state, nor is it in money, nor does it come from the barrel of a gun. Rather, we are empowered to participate whenever we form into congregations that seek to hear and do *torah*; individuals can and should resist injustice, but only in community can we do justice. In an unredeemed world, we are all refugees in need of congregational sanctuary.

But where does this leave unbelievers? Can they, too, enter into full communion with the covenant people that the Christians among us sometimes call the church?

Dom Helder Camara seems to think so. This Catholic bishop who has led in the development of base communities clearly and respectfully invites atheists' unmarginalized participation, and in doing so he expresses the prevailing spirit of covenant ecumenism. But the strongest barriers to the communion of unbelievers are built by unbelievers themselves. History has so fused credal forms with most covenant congregations' faith-and-practice that hypocrisy and repression seem to be the price unbelievers must pay if they are to become communicants. This calls for testimony from an unbeliever to complement the invitation from believers.

As the only unbeliever on the committee that planned the sanctuary symposium, I probably should have suggested a place explicitly for us on the program, although this in itself would be misleading if taken as an indication that suitable niches are unavailable among the Christians, Jews, Quakers, and Unitarians whose congregrations now constitute the sanctuary network. So I'll compensate here by offering a brief testimony concerning my faith—no more than an indication, but maybe enough to point a way for others:

I'm an unbeliever.

That is, I don't believe selfhood survives death, and I consider any conceivable God to be an idol. As I read the Bible, this kind of unbelief is entirely consistent with the faith of Abraham and Moses and achieves classic expression in the Book of Job. Legend has it that Abraham began by smashing idols; in opposition to all the religions of his day, he proclaimed that no object is worthy of worship. Moses showed equal disdain for the consoling speculations of popular religiosity; in contrast to Egyptian religion's obsession with afterlife, the faith that formed Israel is rigorously thisworldly. The Book of Job rejects belief in reward or punishment as a support for the covenant faith; in opposition to the self-serving religion of his friends, Job insists that the person who serves to actualize *shalom* must be ready to suffer.

I'm a true unbeliever, not an atheist or agnostic.

Both the atheist's negation of God's existence and the agnostic's profession of uncertainty about whether God exists presuppose an idolatrous formulation of "God"—a Supreme Being that might or might not exist. A consistent atheist would have no referential basis for recognizing an idol, but most of the atheists I know are Abrahamically conscientious in their observance of the first three commandments. That is, they seem to be unbelievers who think they are atheists. Denying or doubting God's existence is usually an emphatic way of rejecting the idolatries of popular religiosity.

"Whoever rejects idolatry acknowledges the whole of the Torah."[5]

The prophetic faith follows from the rejection of idolatry, not from the formulation and affirmation of some kind of theism. In this, unbelievers may run less risk of distraction than believers. (I would disagree with Helder Camara about substituting "nature" or "evolution" for "God").

But I have no case to make for my unbelief. Rather, I simply wish to emphasize that covenant-based faith bridges differences of creed, rite, and culture and even transcends the division between believers and unbelievers.

The Needle's Eye

"Love must not be a matter of words or talk; it must be genuine and show itself in action."[6] It is not by words but by action that a congregation covenants to serve life. The immediate practical consequence is that the congregation enters into protective community with those who are being violated. This is the place of the serving community, because it is precisely the violated who must become full participants in life if humankind is to become whole. The poor and persecuted are not to replace the rich as the world's owners and consumers. Rather, no part of humanity, or even of life itself, is to be excluded from the total harmony of peace and justice that is *shalom*. If, in some Pauline afterlife, we find ourselves looking down from heaven onto the agonies of hell, our place as a covenant community will be with the damned.

In Latin America, the church's entering into community with the violated is bringing both renewed vitality and a new age of martyrs. This renewal of the covenant is arriving here in Anglo America in person, by way of Salvadoran and Guatemalan refugees. As fugitive "illegals" whose most urgent need is to escape capture, these refugees confront faith communities in the United States with the pivotal choice faced by the Latin American church. We can serve the rule of love, or we can serve the rule of violence. We can serve life as participating co-creators of *shalom*, or we can serve death as consuming possessors of a fractured world of objects. But we must decide one way or the other.

In Latin America, it is the violated themselves who are forming base communities to actualize *shalom*. In Anglo America, the decision for sanctuary opens the way for congregations composed of the beneficiaries of violence to become base communities that also serve. These congregations consider protective community with the persecuted to be integral to the practice of their faith, a matter of serving life rather than violence. The U.S. Justice Department considers it to be a criminal conspiracy, a felony that merits imprisonment. Because genuine communion with the refugees means, then, that we, too, must become "illegals," the decision for sanctuary is definitive. This is rarely the case in our relation to the violated. We are usually blind to their presence and unaware of any need to decide between entering into community with them and rejecting the covenant by maintaining the privileges we inherit from conquest. The decision for sanctuary therefore functions as a pivot point for turning away from conquest and toward congregational growth into full community with the violated. It is, though, an initiation rather than a fruition and is no substitute for the congregation's seeking out its vocation.

The State, the Law, and the Sanctuary Covenant

Because the sanctuary covenant is integral to congregants' practice of their faith rather than to citizens' observance of the law, participants rarely know about the issues of humanitarian and human rights law that are involved. As a result, they often confuse "civil disobedience" that defends established refugee law with civil disobedience directed against unjust laws. The failure to clarify the distinction between refugees and illegal immigrants forfeits recognition of refugee law's relevance to the practice of sanctuary. Awareness of all citizens' legal right and responsibility to protect the victims of persecution is also a casualty of this confusion.

Initially, those of us involved in sanctuary assumed that, as nonviolent direct action that government officials claim is unlawful, sanctuary is a variant of the civil disobedience that matured in the practice and reflection of Thoreau, Gandhi, and King. But our subsequent practice of sanctuary on the border has led to the discovery that, as community with the persecuted, sanctuary is the foundation for peacemaking that is in significant measure outside the range of civil disobedience. Misconceiving sanctuary as a variant form of civil disobedience blinds us to its actual dynamics as a socially constructive practice of our faith.

Widespread awareness of this distinction is now crucial if the provision of sanctuary is to build an institutional foundation for the exercise of local initiative in protecting the victims of state crimes, as required by the Nuremberg Principles. Only if guided by a constructive understanding of the sanctuary covenant's relation to international law will interfaith networking to provide sanctuary for undocumented refugees build a social base from which individuals and communities can, by their own compliance with the law, hold the state accountable for its violation of human rights.

This is possible because sanctuary is rooted in our history. If the sanctuary movement were simply a means for furthering partisan objectives, police repression could destroy it by making it inexpedient. If it were the political tool of a few activists, it could be eliminated by imprisoning them. But because sanctuary for the victims of persecution is inherent in the congregational practice of a deep-rooted and widespread faith, government attack can only intensify the dedication and stimulate the growth of sanctuary covenant communities. Yet, although government attack will, in any case, strengthen rather than weaken the sanctuary movement, if we misconceive sanctuary as civil disobedience that pits faith and morality against law, we will reinforce the state's attempt to nullify our human right and civil duty to take the initiative in protecting the victims of state crimes.

Misconceiving sanctuary as traditional civil disobedience also concedes the disestablishment of a basic religious liberty. The protection of war victims and the persecuted as established by the existing body of humanitarian and human rights law is, in addition to being a civic duty, a practice of our covenant faith. This means that, whenever federal prosecutors succeed in excluding these legal issues from the trial of those involved in providing sanctuary for Central Americans, prosecution constitutes an attack on the established rights of the church itself. Conversely, the government's attack is limited to those involved in the sanctuary movement only if, first, the prosecution has the burden of proof in showing that the Central Americans aided are "illegal aliens" rather than refugees and if, second, the defendants are permitted to present evidence to the jury that the U.S. government's violation of Central American refugees' rights necessitates the provision of sanctuary by covenant communities. In short, whatever various clergy and faith communities may think about the merits of providing sanctuary for Central Americans, the faith community's legitimate social role is denied when a court refuses to permit consideration of humanitarian and human rights law in a sanctuary trial.

The Reagan administration agrees with all other recent administrations that refugees are not illegal immigrants. Elliott Abrams, the assistant secretary of state for human rights and humanitarian affairs, recently put it this way: "Legally and morally, the distinction between economic migrants and political refugees matters greatly. The United States is legally obligated and morally bound to protect refugees but not to accept for permanent residence every illegal immigrant who reaches our shores."[7]

The UN refugee protocol is one of several international laws that establish refugee rights in the United States. It requires signatories to grant asylum to anyone who has "a well-founded fear of being persecuted for reasons of race, religion, nationality, membership in a particular social group, or political opinion." Here is how President Johnson summarized its intent when he submitted it to the Senate for ratification: "Foremost among the humanitarian rights which the Protocol provides is the prohibition against expulsion or return of refugees to any country in which they would face persecution."[8]

Article Fourteen of the Universal Declaration of Human Rights (UDHR) is broader than the Refugee Convention and Protocol, categorically declaring refugee rights for all who flee persecution: "Everyone has the right to seek and to enjoy in other countries asylum from persecution." The UDHR is of special importance as a "Bill of Responsibilities" that, even when unimplemented by the signatory state itself, declares the universality of specific rights for all human beings. Violation of these rights therefore invites the initiative of any private individuals and groups that are capable of taking needed protective action.

The 1949 Geneva Conventions on War and War Victims formulate our obligations to refugees who are fleeing life-threatening armed conflict. The return of war refugees is prohibited until after the cessation of life-threatening hostilities. The furtherance of convention violations that is implicit in the deportation of war refugees to a convention violator is also prohibited. For example, if a civil war is under way in El Salvador and, also, if the armed forces of El Salvador are gross violators of human rights and are known to torture, to murder civilians and captives, or to designate free-fire zones in which artillery or air attacks will result in the massacre of civilians, then the return by the United States government of Salvadorans fleeing the violence is itself a violation of the Geneva Conventions. To prevent signatories from extracting waivers such as the "voluntary departure" coerced by the U.S. government from imprisoned Salvadoran and Guatemalan refugees, the Geneva Conventions also stipulate that in no circumstances may protected persons waive their rights as established by the conventions.

As explained in the *U.N. High Commissioner for Refugees'*

Handbook: "Recognition of his refugee status does not [make a person] a refugee but declares him to be one. He does not become a refugee because of recognition, but is recognized because he is a refugee." International and domestic laws also require observance of the same standards for recognizing refugee status, regardless of a person's race or country of origin.

The responsibility for observing and protecting refugees' right to asylum rests on all of us—not just on government officials. Following the Second World War, the Military Tribunals at Nuremberg established the foundations for this responsibility as follows:

> The essence of the Charter [of the Military Tribunal] is that individuals have international duties that transcend the national obligation of obedience imposed by the individual state.[9]

> International law operates as a restriction and limitation on the sovereignty of nations. It may also limit the obligations which individuals owe to their states, and create for them international obligations which are binding on them to the extent that they must be carried out even if to do so violates a positive law or directive of state.[10]

From the Declaration of Independence to the trials at Nuremberg, our country has recognized that good citizenship requires that we disobey laws or officials whenever they mandate the violation of human rights. A government that commits crimes against humanity forfeits its claim to legitimacy.

The Nuremberg Principles are often dismissed as laws that apply only to the vanquished. This is true if international humanitarian and human rights law is enforced solely by one state against another. But this criticism also has its constructive corollary, as indicated in Justice Jackson's opening statement at the tribunal:

> This principle of personal liability is a necessary as well as logical one if International Law is to render real help to the maintenance of peace. An International Law which operates only on states can be enforced only by war because the most practicable method of coercing a state is warfare.[11]

Unless citizens assume responsibility for complying with international law, war is the primary means of enforcement. Yet, if there is to be peaceful implementation when international law is violated by the state, the citizen's compliance depends on his or her participation in a community that covenants to do justice. This simply points to an unfinished task that was implicit at the tribunal. It proclaimed everyone's right to aid the persecuted but failed to establish a social base for citizens to exercise this right. Sanctuary congregations are now forming that base; from the perspective established by international law, this is exactly what the provision of sanctuary does. Covenant communities' right and duty to protect the victims of government persecution must be conceded by the state if the proceedings at Nuremberg are to have any shred of juridical validity.

If, however, it is up to each covenant community to recognize and then provide sanctuary from government violations of human rights, doesn't this concede the exercise of governmental prerogatives to faith communities?

Good citizenship requires that every individual and community protect the victims of persecution and obstruct the commission of state crimes, but when done openly and nonviolently the provision of sanctuary involves no assumption of state powers. In our Anglo-American approach to self-government, the state can challenge the validity of a community's sanctuary activities by bringing the community's members to trial, and it is then up to a jury to determine whether, in fact, there is a violation of human rights by government officials that justifies the provision of sanctuary. But will the government, through its courts, permit juries to learn about sanctuary issues?

That remains to be seen; yet the verdict will, in any case, still be up to the jury rather than the state. And, if the courts should prevent juries from learning the truth about sanctuary cases or about their responsibility and power to act in the defense of human rights, the public from which juries are drawn will eventually learn from church, press, and other sources.

Many of us will probably serve some time in jail before we reach the day when all juries impaneled to judge a sanctuary case will know that they are deciding whether the violation of human rights by the government necessitates sanctuary. But when that day arrives, a liberty that is essential both for the defense of human rights and for the practice of our covenant faith will be actualized for our country.

Government spokespersons dismiss the endorsement of sanctuary by the mainline religious denominations as the action of misled do-gooders who lack the administration's expert understanding of Latin America—although, when it comes to experience, insight, and current information about Central America, the U.S. Foreign Service is no match for the expertise and networking of the church. The church-led opposition to our government's violation of human rights in Central America is based primarily on personal knowledge rather than reports, which cuts right through the webs of deception spun by politicians and cold warriors.

A similar process takes place regarding refugee policy. For example, in Tucson the community itself has aided thousands of refugees to evade capture and, when refugees are captured, has provided legal services that delay deportation. Of the approximately fifteen hundred Salvadoran asylum applicants provided legal services by the Tucson Ecumenical Council, all have received the State Department's form letter rejection and none has been approved for political asylum. (Just one of the hundreds of Guatemalan applicants who have been aided by the Tucson Ecumenical Council has been granted asylum by an immigration judge. The INS is appealing the decision.) Women who arrive with bullets still in them, men scarred by torture, children emotionally shattered by having been forced to witness the gang rape of their mothers—all are indiscriminately denied asylum in our country.

During recent months, refugees have surged out of El Salvador. They report massacres by the military that are beyond anything previously suffered. Most of these mass murders are perpetrated by aerial attack in areas that are now free-fire zones. The idea is to use military assault to uproot the people and then to force the survivors into "model villages" under strict military supervision. The process is called "pacification." It has become the Pentagon's final solution to the Third World problem.

As the key superpower strategy for using military means to maintain established patterns of rule in the Third World, pacification subordinates refugee aid to military objectives. The violation of refugee rights is integral to the use of this strategy, because military pacification won't work if the refugees it creates have an alternative to the model villages. Given a choice, Salvadorans and Guatemalans are more likely to go to Los Angeles.

Sad to confess, we Anglo Americans seem to share some of the Third Reich's moral insensitivity to technocratically organized mass murder. If unchecked, military pacification of the Third World could become as murderous as the death camps. But all of us are in a position to check it right here at home, where it confronts us in the presence of refugees who need to avoid capture. And, whatever our insensitivities, our churches and synagogues are leading the way by providing sanctuary.

An ongoing violation of refugee rights by federal officials generates a crisis of legitimacy throughout society. For example, the Nuremberg Principles and the Geneva Conventions apply to local governments, prohibiting their law enforcement agencies from collaborating in the violation of refugee rights. Airlines that contract to return refugees and "charities" that contract to imprison them are also violating international law. Church authorities who prevent congregations under their guidance from becoming sanctuaries and university authorities who deny student bodies their right to protect refugees are actively collaborating in the commission of crimes against humanity. Journalists who call refugees illegal aliens are collaborating as propagandists, deadening public awareness of the human rights violations that are occurring.

Press-selected sanctuary spokespersons are commonly asked how they justify "violating the law" in order to shelter "illegal refugees" from the authorities. In the interest of presenting a variety of opinions, journalists also sometimes ask similar questions of uninvolved clergy. Most journalists are unconscious of the glaring lack of professionalism that is implicit in this kind of prosecutorial misstatement, but many sanctuary spokespersons and virtually all uninvolved clergy are equally unaware that, as with sexist and racist language, this usage blinds us to the violation of established human rights. Led by the question's false premise, sanctuary congregants often respond as though their protection of refugees were a practice of the covenant faith—as well as a mandate of basic morality—that conflicts with the requirements of federal law. The crisis of legitimacy is further aggravated as this misconception spreads.

Although there is now no question that international law is binding for everyone—not just for the state—and that citizens are legally obliged to disobey government officials rather than collaborate either actively or passively in the commission of state crimes, courts usually refuse to hold the government accountable to its citizens for its violations of international law. Juries will rarely learn about their Nuremberg responsibilities in court, because the authority and integrity of the judicial system itself is threatened by the crisis of legitimacy generated by a government's committing crimes against humanity. Prophetic witness is then the community's only nonviolent way to hold the state accountable—which means that it is then up to the church to serve as the community's institutional foundation for complying with humanitarian and human rights law. Whatever a faith community may ultimately decide about the provision of sanctuary, this witness begins with the exercise of guidance and teaching responsibilities by the community's pastors and educators.

Whenever a congregation that proclaims the prophetic faith abandons the poor and persecuted to organized violation, its unfaithfulness darkens the way for all humankind. And when it stands as a community's bulwark against state violations of human rights, it lights the way. Sanctuary communities make no claim to a privileged relation to the state and its laws that would exempt them from the responsibilities of good citizenship. To the contrary, the congregational obligation to protect the victims of state crimes extends beyond our individual civic responsibilities, because only in this kind of covenant community can we provide sanctuary for the violated.

By becoming sanctuaries for the violated, congregations composed of the beneficiaries of violence choose to serve life rather than death. Sanctuary is, then, grounded neither in a concession to the church from the state nor in the privileged institutional status of the church's administrative superstructures. Nor is it the cumulative outgrowth of individuals' conscientious objection to state violence. Rather, the congregational practice of sanctuary is grounded here: every covenant congregation is empowered to serve in establishing the earth itself as a sanctuary for all life. Our faith-and-practice as peoples of the covenant is to be the way of hallowing that joins creation's initiating goodness to the harmonious wholeness of *shalom*.

NOTES

1. Helder Camara, *The Desert Is Fertile* (Maryknoll, NY: Orbis Books, 1974), pp. 13-14.

2. Torat Kohanim, 86b, as translated in Solomon Schechter, *Aspects of Rabbinic Theology* (New York: Schocken Books, 1961), p. 133.

3. Exodus 3:14.

4. Cf. Martin Buber, *The Way of Man According to the Teaching of Hasidism* (Seacaucus, NJ: Citadel Press, 1966), p. 17.

5. Sifre on Numbers, 111:32a; Chullin 5a.

6. 1 John 3:18.

7. Elliott Abrams, "U.S. Refugee Policy Is Nothing to Flee," *Los Angeles Times* (17 Jan. 1985), part 2, p. 5.

8. Public papers of the President of the United States, Lyndon B. Johnson, 1968–69, book 2, p. 869 (Washington, D.C.: U.S. Government Printing Office, 1970).

9. *United States v. Goering*, Judgement of the International Military Tribunal, 6F.R.D. 69, 110 (1946).

10. *United States v. Von Leeb*, Judgement of U.S. Military Tribunal #V, 27 October 1948.

11. *The Nürnberg Case as Presented by Robert H. Jackson* (New York: Cooper Square Publishers, 1971), p. 88.

APPENDIX: RESOURCES ON BEGINNING AND MAINTAINING SANCTUARY

Sanctuary is the offering of protection to political refugees denied asylum by the U.S. government. It is a public affirmation of support for people whose lives would be threatened if they were forced to return to their homeland. The typical provider of sanctuary is a church or synagogue congregation, but it can be any community of faith—faith being understood in the broadest sense as a commitment to human rights and moral values. Thus, sanctuary is being offered not only by Campus Christian Centers, Newman Centers, and other church-related groups, but by such secular groups as Campus Sanctuary Committees, and by cities, including Berkeley, California, and Cambridge, Massachusetts.

The sanctuary movement is precisely that—a movement. It is not a juridic entity with centralized decision-making machinery. Participation is by consensus. The nature of the movement leaves various gray areas at its margin. Some have argued that it should be an exclusively religious movement, not open to secular participation. A meeting of sanctuary leaders from around the United States in June 1984 gave this answer:

We agreed that groups participating in Sanctuary—whether religious or secular—must be those for whom Sanctuary is deeply rooted in their tradition and heritage. By reaching back into our roots, we more sharply define ourselves, our identity, and gain a degree of authenticity that is imperative as we journey into the Sanctuary Movement. Unless the declaration of Sanctuary is rooted in tradition, it has the great potential of being a weak decision with a diffuse identity. We must not be exclusive but we must include others with great care and clarity. We must also recognize that the church is not a vanguard movement. Sanctuary, in terms of the history and tradition of the church, is a unique expression of church solidarity. It is a dynamic movement that is no longer just place but more than place, an event and a community.[1]

Two observations are pertinent. First, this or any ruling is not binding, given the absence of a juridical decision-making body. Besides, the concept of sanctuary is rooted in the U.S. secular tradition no less than in the Judeo-Christian religious tradition—suffice to recall the sanctuary from the agents of Charles II provided by the New Haven community to two refugees from England being sought because they had signed the death warrant of Charles I.

Sanctuary at first was thought of almost exclusively as the providing of living space and a support community for a refugee or refugee family. The concept has significantly broadened in response to experience. Though there is a core group now consisting of considerably more than two hundred churches and synagogues (and a half dozen secular university campuses), the support community number in the thousands. Some communities support one of their members to work for a period with refugees near the Mexican border, a commitment that frequently leads to a formal declaration of sanctuary for refugees with whom their representative has worked. Another alternative is to bond out from an INS detention center and initiate proceedings for political asylum for a refugee or a family for whom the harsh life of these centers has become physically or emotionally intolerable. In this last instance, the INS recognizes that the alien is legally in the country as long as a final negative determination on the asylum claim has not been made. The process may take many years.

To declare sanctuary is a serious decision. The reasons that justify challenging the current administration's interpretation of the law must be understood. They have been adequately presented in the pages of this book and need not be repeated here. The legal risks and other elements to be evaluated are set out in this appendix. It is essential that the entire community (congregation) reach a consensus before declaring sanctuary. Action by a small group on its own or even by a small majority in a reluctant community is divisive and will not provide a positive atmosphere for the refugees. At least two-thirds should strongly favor the action. The decision should come from a faith commitment. The question the community must address is, What is our duty as people of faith?

Decision making varies by denomination. The formalities of the process are determined by the practice of the denomination or community and the local circumstances. Before coming to a decision, however, much advance work usually is necessary.

The first step is to create an organizing committee. It may be an existing social concerns or peace and justice committee of the congregation, a Central American solidarity group, or an ad hoc body. Membership should be as broad as possible, with at least four or five committed persons willing to devote considerable time. The initiators should list all local churches, synagogues, and other communities that are potential sponsors of a sanctuary in order of their probable willingness to participate. Elements to be taken into account include previous concern with Central America, seminars or talks on Central American issues, social activism, public stands by clergy on community issues, sponsorship of refugees from other countries. Having selected three or four, the committee should identify key people in each, the pastor, the rabbi, heads of social concern committees, and so on, then determine which committee member should approach each of these.

In addition to a sponsoring congregation, as many other congregations and communities in the neighborhood as possible should be canvassed to become public supporters. Their material aid may be important, as well as their moral support. Many such supporters, if actively involved, end by declaring themselves sanctuaries.

If the organizing committee is a solidarity or an ad hoc group without previous contacts with the religious community, a sanctuary proposal can serve as an introduction. If the committee has no direct contact with potential congregations, a first step might be to offer speakers and educational presentations on Central America and use the opportunity to raise the idea of sanctuary.

Unless the particular congregation is already actively concerned, informal preliminary work should precede a formal proposal to consider declaring sanctuary. Briefings with the key members should include the sharing of materials, news clippings, and stories of the experiences of refugees. They should also make clear that the U.S.

administration regards providing sanctuary as a violation of the law, exposing all involved to prosecution and serious penalties if the courts uphold the administration's view (details later).

The experience of one church, as described by the Rev. David Chevrier, gives a sense of how the decision making develops:

Wellington Avenue Church was first approached by the Chicago Religious Task Force on Central America (CRTFCA) to endorse the sanctuary at Southside Presbyterian Church in Tucson. The Church Council did this and then the CRTFCA approached us about becoming a host congregation. What went into making this decision? The primary thing that went into it was trust that the congregation was mature enough and concerned enough to be allowed to make the decision, one way or the other. Overcoming the anxieties of the leadership (lay and clergy) was a major obstacle. In my experience the anxieties of the leadership over what might be said and how emotions will be handled during the decision-making process are totally out of proportion to the reality. People are capable of making decisions when 1. Opportunities to raise all the questions are provided. These opportunities included: (a) presentations and discussion at meetings of the governing body, council, or board; (b) presentations and discussion at an informational meeting of the congregation when a vote is taken. 2. Adequate information is provided: material on the historical and political situation in Central America, the legal situation and consequences, theological and biblical background of sanctuary, financial cost, and support for such a project. 3. People feel they are taken seriously and listened to. It is important before and during the decision-making process that there are people who are committed to the idea of sanctuary and are willing to work if the congregation decides to do it. The pastor and two or three key laypeople must be committed to it and willing to be legally liable if the INS (Immigration and Naturalization Service) or the Attorney General prosecutes. Three or four people must be willing to put in six to ten hours a week for the first two months on coordinating, food, furniture, clothing, and monitoring, three or four people who are bilingual. Not all of these people need to be in the congregation.[2]

After a congregation has decided to declare sanctuary, much planning and work are still required before it is ready to receive a refugee family. A core committee of five to ten persons should be formed. It is essential that at least one person be fluent in Spanish and be available or easily reachable at all times. The members must be prepared to give considerable time until the family is well established. That usually means six to ten hours weekly for each member, and probably twenty for the coordinator. Not all members need to be from the sponsoring congregation. It is better to have some from other congregations, thus facilitating the objective of maximum involvement of the entire community. The best security for public sanctuary, regardless of the political climate, is widespread public support and publicity.

Once the decisions are made, preparations for the reception of a refugee family begin. The refugees should stay in the church building for one or two weeks, giving them an opportunity to feel secure and also permitting an assessment of how the INS will react. Monitors must be continuously present on the church premises during this period. As soon as the refugees feel emotionally secure, they can move to a house or apartment rented by the organizing committee. It should have a telephone, and emergency telephone numbers and numbers of key sponsorship team members should be provided.

Selection of an appropriate refugee family should begin as soon as the decision to declare sanctuary has been made. The role of this family will involve active and continuing dialogue with the host community, educating as many North Americans as possible about the situation in Central America, about the plight of the refugees there and here, and about U.S. policy toward Central America and toward refugees from Central America. The sanctuary organization for the region in which the sponsoring congregation is located should be approached to help in finding a suitable family. The addresses and telephone numbers for each of the regions are listed later in this appendix.

The sponsoring congregation is responsible for the family until it is economically and emotionally independent. The normal experience is that by that time a bond of permanent friendship has been established. The length of time needed for economic independence will depend to a large extent on the ability of the sponsoring congregation to find suitable work. The refugees will not have working papers and consequently cannot get Social Security cards, without which many firms will not employ them. However, there is no law against anyone working in the United States. There is no law against paying a worker. There is no law against receiving payment for work done. In many situations, the concrete problems can be resolved by having the refugees work as independent contractors.

In making its financial plans, the sponsoring congregation should assume that it will have to take care of the immediate physical needs of the refugees for food, clothing, health care (all of which can usually be obtained through contributions of goods and services), and housing. Total support must continue until receipt of the first paychecks, and rent should be paid for three months. The level of support should be phased down as quickly as possible. It is important to avoid the development of dependency by not providing anything the refugees are able to provide for themselves. It is also necessary to have access to the required cash and collateral to provide bail for each family member in case of detention by the INS. The amount of the bond varies considerably, and the regional sanctuary organization should be consulted. Each congregation should be able to find legal counsel willing to donate services.

A public inauguration ceremony should be planned to welcome the refugee family. If the city has a federal building, it would be appropriate to arrange a candlelight procession or motorcade from this building to the host congregation for a worship service. Sample worship materials are available from the Chicago Religious Task Force. Every effort should be made for coverage by TV, radio, and the press. Normally, it is better not to involve the press until some days before the arrival of the refugees. Presence of reporters during the decision making can be intimidating for many.

Not infrequently, the emotional problems of the refugees are more complicated than the economic. Dr. Laura Bonaparte, an Argentine psychiatrist whose husband and several family members were "disappeared" in Argentina in the early 1970s, is an expert on the emotional problems of exile.

It is a form of torture. One leaves one's history behind and is separated from homeland, family history, and neighbors. And for the family members of those who have been "disappeared" there is another factor; one never thinks that the disappeared is really dead. And we all have instilled in us a warrior spirit; that one must die on the battlefield and not abandon it—or must sink with the ship. We know that these are values of authoritarian societies, but we still carry them in us. The psychology of the political refugee or exile is complex.

Another thing that can be very humiliating for refugees—especially those who have been active in the struggles of their people—is the sense that the groups offering aid are requiring them to adapt. They may react violently, indicating their own desire to adapt and forget, to erase the memory of everything and start all over again, which is what the torturers always require. The issue of collaboration/assimilation is then transferred to the groups offering aid. The refugee seeks to adapt at all costs in order to avoid feelings of guilt, depression, anxiety. There is an ambivalence between the desire to adapt and begin a new life and not to adapt because one is the product of a whole history of struggle and must return.[3]

The psychological effects that are not expressed physically can be the hardest ones to understand. The most serious of these is psychopathology—destructive behavior toward the refugee community. This behavior, which is often justified with political rationalizations, can include robbery, aggression, rumors, gossip, the desire to break up the group—a group that, because of conditions of confusion and trauma, is still very sensitive. Next in terms of seriousness is melancholy, because of the risk of suicide. Melancholic suicide can either be active or can take the form of just letting oneself die. A melancholic person lacks an active attitude, and people end up putting him or her to the side. The way in which melancholy can be destructive to the group of refugees is when it takes the form of mania. The manic person says, "Let's go do this; let's go do that." He or she is hyperactive, cannot stop talking, constantly seeks sexual contacts, and so on. The other reaction is paranoia, through which one's internal feelings are projected onto those around. The paranoid person is always thinking that there is another intention behind any action. Those working directly with newly arrived refugees must be alert to such signs and have available the professional personnel to deal with them.

Reference has already been made to the legal issues raised by the sanctuary movement. Both sanctuary workers and refugees must have a basic understanding of what is involved, while realizing that it is essential to have access to legal counsel if problems arise.

The INS, following administration policy, refuses to recognize that Central Americans have a well-founded fear of persecution that entitles them to political asylum under the UN Convention on Refugees and the U.S. Refugee Act of 1980. Neither does it recognize the right not to be returned to their homeland under the convention and the 1980 act, and also under the 1949 Geneva Conventions on War and War Victims. The refusal of the administration to recognize the legitimacy of their claims to refugee status under U.S. and international law does not render their presence unlawful. The position of the sanctuary movement is that what it is doing is lawful. It may, however, be years before the courts make a definitive ruling. In the meantime, all sanctuary workers and refugees are subject to prosecution. So far, only two have been convicted, Jack Elder and Stacey Merkt, and the convictions are being appealed. Others have been indicted and await trial.

Charges to which sanctuary workers expose themselves include importing or attempting to import an undocumented alien, harboring, transporting, aiding and abetting, and conspiracy. Convictions carry heavy penalties, for example, up to five years' imprisonment and a $10,000 fine for conspiracy, the charge that is usually the easiest to prove.

Undocumented aliens also are liable to criminal charges for entering the United States illegally, the penalty for the first offense being a fine of not more than $500 or imprisonment up to six months, or both. No criminal charges have been pressed against Central Americans in sanctuary. Those arrested in January 1985 were released on bond when they filed applications for political asylum.

Sanctuary congregations who form part of a particular denomination or national religious body will usually have the support of that body in a crisis. Following is a list of central contact points for some major religious bodies. A church or synagogue affiliated with one of these might notify the contact when it decides to declare sanctuary. Also listed are the addresses and telephone numbers of the Sanctuary Regional Centers and written and audiovisual materials that present additional information useful to all involved in the sanctuary movement.

Sanctuary Regional Centers

Northwest: University Baptist Church
4554 12th NE
Seattle, WA 98105
(206) 632-5188

Northern California: East Bay Sanctuary Covenant
                     Newman Hall, Holy Spirit Parish
                     2700 Dwight Way
                     Berkeley, CA 94704
                     (415) 848-7812

Southern California: Interfaith Task Force on Central America
                     1010 S. Flower Street #404
                     Los Angeles, CA 90015
                     (213) 470-2293

North Central: Sanctuary Project
                     c/o AFSC, 1660 Lafayette
                     Denver, CO 80218
                     (303) 832-4508

North Midwest: Madison Sanctuary Committee
                     1121 University Avenue
                     Madison, WI 53715
                     (608) 251-4805

South Midwest: Chicago Religious Task Force on Central America
                     407 S. Dearborn Street, Room 370
                     Chicago, IL 60605
                     (312) 663-4398

Southwest: TEC Task Force for Central America
                     317 W. 23rd Street
                     Tucson, AZ 85713
                     (602) 628-7525

Texas: Metroplex Sanctuary Organizing Committee
                     4906 Bonnie View
                     Dallas, TX 75241
                     (214) 375-3715

Northeast: Sanctuary Education Committee
                     c/o AFSC, 2161 Massachusetts Avenue
                     Cambridge, MA 02140
                     (617) 661-6130

East Central: D.C. Sanctuary Committee
                1470 Irving Street, NW
                Washington, DC 20010
                (202) 332-0292
Border States: Saint William Sanctuary
                1226 W. Oak Street
                Louisville, KY 40210
                (502) 491-0052

South: Common Ground
        546 Bienville Street
        Baton Rouge, LA 70806
        (504) 387-4540

Reading List

SANCTUARY

Sanctuary: A Justice Ministry
Public Sanctuary for Salvadoran and Guatemalan Refugees: Organizer's Nuts and Bolts
Legal Handbook for the Sanctuary Movement
Basta: Supplement #1
   Available from the Chicago Religious Task Force on Central
   America, 407 S. Dearborn Street, Room 370, Chicago, IL 60605;
   (312) 663-4398. $3.00 each, 10 or more copies are $1.50 each
   plus postage.

Seeking Safe Haven—a congregational guide to helping Central
Americans in the United States.
   Available from Church World Service, Immigration and Refugee
   Program, 475 Riverside Drive, Room 656, New York, NY 10115;
   (212) 870-3274. $6.00 per copy.

The Church and Asylum Seekers—study/action packet including
guidelines on providing sanctuary, education, and advocacy, and on
providing medical care and legal assistance to asylum seekers.
   Available from Office of World Service/World Hunger, Presbyterian Center, 341 Ponce de Leon Avenue NE, Atlanta, GA

30365; (404) 873-1531 or from WRERS, 475 Riverside Drive, Room 1268, New York, NY 10115; (212) 870-3290. Free.

No Promised Land: American Refugee Policies and the Rule of Law, by Gary MacEoin and Nivita Riley, 1982, 105 pages. Drawing on the experience of Central American refugees, explores the contradictions of U.S. refugee policy.
  Available from Oxfam America, 115 Broadway Avenue, Boston, · MA 02116; (617) 482-1211. $2.50 each plus 50¢ postage.

Salvadorans in the United States: The Case for Extended Voluntary Departure, American Civil Liberties Union, December 1983.
  Available from Center for National Security Studies, 122 Maryland Avenue NE, Washington, DC 20002; (202) 544-5380. $2.00 per copy.

Sanctuary Bibliography
  Available from the Tucson Ecumenical Council, 317 West 23rd Street, Tucson, AZ 85713; (602) 628-7525. 50¢ per copy.

Summary of Presbyterian General Assembly Actions on Sanctuary
  Available from Douglas Brian, Room 1254, 475 Riverside Drive, New York, NY 10115; (212) 870-2919. Free.

CENTRAL AMERICA

Adventure and Hope: Christians and the Crisis in Central America—a report to the 195th General Assembly (1983) of the Presbyterian Church (U.S.A.).
  Available from the Office of World Service/World Hunger, Division of Corporate and Social Mission, 341 Ponce de Leon Avenue NE, Atlanta, GA 30365; (404) 873-1531 or from the Advisory Council on Church and Society, Room 1020, 475 Riverside Drive, New York, NY 10115; (202) 870-3028.

Changing Course: Blueprint for Peace in Central America and the Caribbean
  Available from the Institute for Policy Studies, 1901 Q Street NW, Washington, DC 20009; (202) 234-9382. 116 pages, $5.00.

Cry of the People: The Struggle for Human Rights in Latin America—the Catholic Church in Conflict with U.S. Policy, by Penny Lernoux.
Penguin Books, 1982, 552 pages. $6.95.

Weakness and Deceit: U.S. Policy and El Salvador, by Raymond Bonner, correspondent for *The New York Times*. Bonner explores the failure of U.S. foreign policy in El Salvador.
Times Books, 1984, 408 pages, $16.95.

Salvador, by Joan Didion. An illuminating description of that country based on firsthand observation and experience.
Washington Square Press, 1983, 108 pages, $5.95.

Bitter Fruit: The Untold Story of the American Coup in Guatemala, by Stephen Kinzer and Stephen Schlesinger. A stunning documentary report based largely on information obtained from government sources under the Freedom of Information Act.
Anchor Press/Doubleday, 1983, 336 pages, $8.95.

"The Struggle for Life in Central America," *Church & Society*, March/April 1983. Reports on task force visits to Central America, U.S. certification for military aid, and providing sanctuary for refugees.
Available from Presbyterian Distribution Service, 935 Interchurch Center, 475 Riverside Drive, New York, NY 10115; (202) 870-2775. $2.00 per copy, PDS #803-01-832.

Audiovisuals

SANCTUARY

The New Underground Railroad—30-minute color video cassette or 16-mm film. Traces the journey of a family in El Salvador to sanctuary in the U.S.; documents the process by which the host congregation in Madison, Wisconsin, decides to declare sanctuary. Rental $30.00, purchase $175.00.
Available from Audio-Visual Center, Indiana University, Bloomington, IN 47405; (812) 335-8087. Also available for short-term

use from Douglas Brian, Program Agency, Room 1254, 475 Riverside Drive, New York, NY 10115; (212) 870-2919.

In Pursuit of Refuge—30-minute slide/tape presentation about people forced to leave El Salvador and Guatemala. Rental $25.00 per week, purchase $65.00.
   Available from The Resource Center, PO Box 4726, Albuquerque, NM 87196; (505) 266-5009.

Sanctuary—58-minute, 16-mm color film about refugees around the world. Rental $12.00 plus shipping costs.
   Available from Presbyterian Film Distribution Centers and Ecufilm, 810 Twelfth Avenue South, Nashville, TN 37203; (800) 251-4091.

El Salvador: Nowhere to Run—30-minute videotape about Salvadoran refugees who have fled the violence of their war-torn country. Rental $25.00.
   Available from Oxfam America, 1154 Broadway Avenue, Boston, MA 02116; (617) 482-1222.

An Act of Subversive Love—20-minute, 16-mm color film on the ministry of sanctuary for Central American refugees in North American churches. A suggested procedure for showing accompanies the film. Rental $20.00, purchase $200.00.
   Available from Peace/Justice Center of Southern California, 2130 East First Street, Los Angeles, CA 90033-3993; (213) 265-3303.

Voices of the Voiceless—30-minute, ½″ VHS videotape, narrated by Mike Farrel. Addresses the conditions of refugees in Los Angeles and the conditions from which they have fled.
   Available from El Rescate, 1813 West Pico Boulevard, Los Angeles, CA 90006; (213) 387-3284.

Central Americans: Know Your Rights—30-minute, ½″ VHS videotape in Spanish, prepared for refugees.
   Available from El Rescate, 1813 West Pico Boulevard, Los Angeles, CA 90006; (213) 387-3284.

Sanctuary: A Question of Conscience—30-minute color video cassette (½" VHS) VIDEO ONE production of the Communications Unit of the Presbyterian Church (USA). Deals with the confrontation between church and state regarding the harboring of Central American refugees. Church and lay leaders speak out on the issue.

Available for short-term use from Douglas Brian, Program Agency, Room 1254, 475 Riverside Drive, New York, NY 10115; (212) 870-2919. No charge.

CENTRAL AMERICA

Americans in Transition—29-minute, 16-mm color film, 1981. Depicts U.S. involvement in Latin America, particularly Central America, during this century. Ed Asner narrates.

Available for use from Office of Community Development, Program Agency, Room 1254, 475 Riverside Drive, New York, NY 10115; (212) 870-2919.

Central America: Roots of the Crisis—28-minute color slide show with cassette tape, 1981. Outlines the history, politics, and economics of the situation.

Available for use from Office of Community Development, Program Agency, Room 1254, 475 Riverside Drive, New York, NY 10115; (212) 870-2919.

Witness to the Slaughter: The Church in Guatemala—23-minute color filmstrip with cassette tape. Deals with the current violence in Guatemala.

Available for use from Office of Community Development, Program Agency, Room 1254, 475 Riverside Drive, New York, NY 10115; (212) 870-2919.

Born from the People: Toward Understanding Central America—22-minute color filmstrip with cassette tape. Presents the causes of the present crisis in Central America. $15.00 per set.

Available from the Office of World Service/World Hunger, Division of Corporate and Social Mission, 341 Ponce de Leon Avenue NE, Atlanta, GA 30365; (404) 873-1531.

For additional information on documentaries dealing with sanctuary or with Central America, contact Media Network, 208 W 13 Street, New York, NY 10011. (212) 620-0877.

NOTES TO APPENDIX

1. Meeting of Sanctuary activists, Tucson, AZ, 21–22 June 1984. Minutes prepared by Eileen Purcell, Catholic Social Services, San Francisco.
2. *Sanctuary: A Justice Ministry* (Chicago: Religious Task Force on Central America, 1983), p. 15.
3. Personal communication to Gary MacEoin in September 1984.

CONTRIBUTORS

MARTA BENAVIDES, a Salvadoran, is an ordained Baptist minister. In 1978 Archbishop Oscar Romero named her Director of the Ecumenical Committee for Humanitarian Aid for the Archdiocese of San Salvador, where she worked closely with the archbishop until his assassination in March 1980. She has since been Director of MEDEPAZ (Pennsylvania), an ecumenical agency working for peace and development in El Salvador.

ANGELA BERRYMAN is a Central American specialist in the Peace Education Division of the American Friends Service Committee. From 1976 to 1980 she served as Central American Representative, with headquarters in Guatemala, for the American Friends Service Committee. A graduate in biology, she worked in Huehuetenango, Guatemala, from 1968 to 1970, and in a barrio in Panama from 1970 to 1973. She has traveled extensively throughout Latin America.

ROBERT MCAFEE BROWN, Professor of Theology and Ethics, Pacific School of Religion, Berkeley, California, holds a master's degree from Union Theological Seminary and a doctorate from Columbia University. He has taught at Union Theological Seminary, Macalester College, and Stanford University. Author of more than twenty books, he is on the boards of the Institute for Advanced Religious Studies, Jerusalem, and the U.S. Holocaust Memorial Council.

MARILYN CHILCOTE, a Presbyterian minister, is Director of the East Bay Sanctuary Covenant, Berkeley, California. A participant in the first declaration of sanctuary in March 1982, she has traveled extensively in Central America, organizing a visitor program to protect Salvadorans in refugee camps in Honduras from attacks by Salvadoran military forces and death squads. This program, maintaining a continuous presence of North Americans in the major camps, and involving altogether more than 200 people, is now in its third year.

WILLIAM SLOANE COFFIN, pastor of Riverside Church, New York, joined the CIA in 1950 and for three years trained anti-Soviet Russians for operation inside the Soviet Union. A graduate of the Yale Divinity School, he was chaplain at Yale University for eighteen years. He attained national prominence as an opponent of the Vietnam War, and he is equally identified for his opposition to U.S. policy in Central America.

JIM CORBETT is a Quaker "unbeliever." Originally from Wyoming, he studied philosophy at Colgate (B.A.'54) and Harvard (M.A. '55) and then, during most of the succeeding thirty years, has lived on the Sonoran desert of Arizona as a cowboy, goatherd, and rancher. He has also worked as a sheepherder, Forest Service range analyst, Park Service ranger, horse trader, librarian, and teacher of wildland symbiotics. Crippled by arthritis, he now lives in Tucson, supported by his wife, Pat, an agricultural worker specializing in arid lands crops.

YVONNE DILLING, Director of Witness for Peace in Washington, D.C., majored in Peace Studies and Conflict Resolution, specializing in Latin America, at Manchester College, Indiana. An ordained minister of the Church of the Brethren, she worked for eighteen months with the Caritas relief agency in Salvadoran refugee camps in Honduras. This experience is the subject of her book, *In Search of Refuge*.

JOHN H. ELLIOTT is Professor of Theology and Religious Studies at the University of San Francisco, the first Lutheran to teach theology at this Jesuit university. With a doctorate in theology from the Vestfalische Wilhelms' Universitat, Germany, he teaches graduate and undergraduate courses that emphasize the interdisciplinary and ecumenical perspectives of the study of religion.

RENNY GOLDEN is coauthor with Michael McConnell of *Sanctuary and the Underground Railroad* (Maryknoll, NY: Orbis Books, Fall 1985). She teaches in the Crime and Social Justice Department at

Northeastern Illinois University. She initiated an Adult Base Education Program incorporating Paulo Freire's method in the black/ Latino communities of Chicago's West Side. She has a doctorate of ministry from Chicago Theological Seminary.

FELIPE IXCOT JALBEN, an indigenous Mayan-Quiché Indian from an extremely poor family in Guatemala, is married and has five children. He left school after the fourth grade and worked as a *campesino* (farmer) and a catechist. Marked as a subversive for teaching the gospel to fellow *campesinos*, he fled to the United States and now lives in sanctuary at Weston Priory, Vermont, a Benedictine monastery.

GARY MACEOIN is a self-employed writer with a doctorate in Spanish Language and Literature from the National University of Ireland. He is also a lawyer. Since the 1940s he has specialized in Latin American affairs and has visited Central America nine times since 1980. His more than twenty books include *Revolution Next Door: Latin America in the 1970s.*

MURDO J. MACLEOD, Professor of History, University of Arizona, has a master's degree in Spanish and French Language and Literature from the University of Glasgow, Scotland, and a doctorate in Inter-American Studies (History), with additional study in sociology and political science from the University of Florida. He has studied and taught for extended periods in Central and South America.

MARSHALL T. MEYER is Vice President of the University of Judaism, Los Angeles. A native of New York, he studied at Columbia University, the Hebrew University (Jerusalem), and the Jewish Theological Seminary of America. For twenty years he worked in Argentina as an editor, professor of theology, and rabbi and was a member of the Argentine National Commission Concerning Disappeared Persons.

REV. FRANCIS XAVIER MURPHY is a writer-in-residence and lecturer at Holy Redeemer College, Washington, D.C. With a doctorate in Medieval History from the Catholic University of America, he taught patristic studies at a Roman university for many years. More recently he was a Fellow at the Woodrow Wilson International Center for Scholars, studying World Problems of Growth.

DAVIE NAPIER was born in China and educated in China, Japan, and the United States. A graduate of Yale Divinity School, he holds a doctorate from Yale University. He has taught at Alfred University, New York, the University of Georgia, Yale Divinity School, Stanford University, and Pacific School of Religion. A biblical scholar, his specialization is the Pentateuch. His many books include *Come, Sweet Death* and *Prophets in Perspective*.

JAMES W. NICKEL is Professor of Philosophy and Director of the Center for Study of Values and Social Policy at the University of Colorado. With a doctorate in philosophy from the University of Kansas he has concentrated his teaching and research on social, political, and legal philosophy, and he is Project Director for a major study, "Value and Policy Issues in Science and Technology."

HERB SCHMIDT is pastor of the community of Christ Lutheran, University of Arizona, a graduate of St. Paul's College, Concordia, Missouri, and Concordia Seminary, St. Louis. He did postgraduate work at Washington University, Pacific Lutheran Theological Seminary, and San Francisco Theological Seminary. Previous posts include Campus Pastor at the University of California, Santa Cruz, and Assistant Dean of Studies at California Concordia College, Oakland. He is President of the Southern Arizona Hunger Action Center in Tucson, Arizona.

GUS SCHULTZ, a bishop of the Association of Evangelical Lutheran Churches, is a campus minister at the University of California at Berkeley. He played a key role in creating a sanctuary for service men who were conscientious objectors during the Vietnam War and in having the City of Berkeley declare itself a sanctuary for them. He has played and plays a similar role in the sanctuary movement for Central Americans.

RICHARD SHAULL is Henry Luce Professor of Ecumenics, Emeritus, at Princeton Theological Seminary. He has spent more than twenty years as a missionary teacher in Brazil, Colombia, and other Latin American countries. His most recent book, *Heralds of a New Reformation* (Maryknoll, NY: Orbis Books, 1984), deals with Latin American Theology of Liberation and the emerging Church of the Poor.

ELSA TAMEZ, a Mexican, studied in Costa Rica and holds graduate degrees in theology, literature, and language. She teaches Old Testament and Greek at the Latin American Biblical Seminary in Costa Rica, and she is the author of several books and articles on biblical reinterpretation and on the status of women. Her *Bible of the Oppressed* has been translated into English, French, Dutch, and Portuguese.

JIM WALLIS, founder and pastor of Sojourners Community, Washington, D.C., is Editor of *Sojourners* magazine, a preacher, an activist, and the author of several books. Involved in civil rights and antiwar struggles since the late 1960s, he designed "A Pledge of Resistance," a nationwide contingency plan for massive civil disobedience in the event of a U.S. invasion of Central America.

PHILIP WHEATON, an Episcopal priest, is director of Ecumenical Program for Inter-american Communication and Action (EPICA), located in Washington, D.C. EPICA focuses on socio-economic problems and political struggles in Central America and the Caribbean, with emphasis on the U.S. role in the region. Wheaton spent some ten years as a missionary in the Dominican Republic.

ELIE WIESEL is Andrew W. Mellon Professor in the Humanities and Professor of Religion at Boston University, a survivor of Auschwitz and Buchenwald, and for many years a stateless person. He is recognized as the leading historian of the Holocaust. His more than twenty published books include novels, autobiography, plays, and philosophic essays. He is himself the subject of at least a dozen books.

WILLIAM L. WIPFLER is Director of the Human Rights Office, Division of Overseas Ministry, of the National Council of Churches. He worked as a pastor and professor of theology for eleven years in the Dominican Republic and Costa Rica, after which he spent ten years as head of the Caribbean and Latin American department of the National Council of Churches. He has a doctorate from Union Theological Seminary.